Devil's Advocates

DEVIL'S ADVOCATES is a series of books devoted to exploring the classics of horror cinema. Contributors to the series come from the fields of teaching, academia, journalism and fiction, but all have one thing in common: a passion for the horror film and a desire to share it with the widest possible audience.

'The admirable Devil's Advocates series is not only essential – and fun – reading for the serious horror fan but should be set texts on any genre course.'
Dr Ian Hunter, Reader in Film Studies, De Montfort University, Leicester

'Auteur Publishing's new Devil's Advocates critiques on individual titles... offer bracingly fresh perspectives from passionate writers. The series will perfectly complement the BFI archive volumes.' **Christopher Fowler,** *Independent on Sunday*

'Devil's Advocates has proven itself more than capable of producing impassioned, intelligent analyses of genre cinema... quickly becoming the go-to guys for intelligent, easily digestible film criticism.' ***Horror Talk.com***

'Auteur Publishing continue the good work of giving serious critical attention to significant horror films.' ***Black Static***

 DevilsAdvocatesbooks

DevilsAdBooks

ALSO AVAILABLE IN THIS SERIES

A Girl Walks Home Alone at Night Farshid Kazemi

Black Sunday Martyn Conterio

The Blair Witch Project Peter Turner

Blood and Black Lace Roberto Curti

The Blood on Satan's Claw David Evans-Powell

Candyman Jon Towlson

Cannibal Holocaust Calum Waddell

Carrie Neil Mitchell

The Company of Wolves James Gracey

The Conjuring Kevin J. Wetmore, Jr.

Creepshow Simon Brown

Cruising Eugenio Ercolani & Marcus Stiglegger

The Curse of Frankenstein Marcus K. Harmes

Daughters of Darkness Kat Ellinger

Dead of Night Jez Conolly & David Bates

The Descent James Marriot

The Devils Darren Arnold

Don't Look Now Jessica Gildersleeve

The Fly Emma Westwood

Frenzy Ian Cooper

Halloween Murray Leeder

House of Usher Evert Jan van Leeuwen

In the Mouth of Madness Michael Blyth

It Follows Joshua Grimm

Ju-on The Grudge Marisa Hayes

Let the Right One In Anne Billson

M Samm Deighan

Macbeth Rebekah Owens

The Mummy Doris V. Sutherland

Nosferatu Cristina Massaccesi

Peeping Tom Kiri Bloom Walden

Saw Benjamin Poole

Scream Steven West

The Shining Laura Mee

Shivers Luke Aspell

The Silence of the Lambs Barry Forshaw

Suspiria Alexandra Heller-Nicholas

The Texas Chain Saw Massacre James Rose

The Thing Jez Conolly

Twin Peaks: Fire Walk With Me Lindsay Hallam

Witchfinder General Ian Cooper

FORTHCOMING

[REC] Jim Harper

The Conjuring Kevin Wetmore

The Evil Dead Lloyd Haynes

Repulsion Jeremy Carr

DEVIL'S ADVOCATES

TROUBLE EVERY DAY

KATE ROBERTSON

First published in 2021 by
Auteur, an imprint of
Liverpool University Press,
4 Cambridge Street,
Liverpool
L69 7ZU

Series design: Nikki Hamlett at Cassels Design
Set by Cassels Design

All rights reserved. No part of this publication may be reproduced in any material form (including photocopying or storing in any medium by electronic means and whether or not transiently or incidentally to some other use of this publication) without the permission of the copyright owner.

Figures from *Trouble Every Day* are © ARTE / Arte France Cinéma / Canal+.

British Library Cataloguing-in-Publication Data
A catalogue record for this book is available from the British Library

ISBN paperback: 978-1-80085-925-8
ISBN hardback: 978-1-80085-924-1
ISBN epub: 978-1-80085-807-7
ISBN PDF: 978-1-80034-396-2

Contents

1 Introduction: Why *Trouble Every Day?* 7

2 An Inventory of Images: Assembling an Elliptical Narrative 25

3 Borders/Bodies: Space, Surface, Touch and Desire 55

4 Situating the Film: References and Lineage 81

5 The Legacy of *Trouble Every Day* 101

Acknowledgements 105

Bibliography 107

1. INTRODUCTION: WHY *TROUBLE EVERY DAY*?

> For me, the monster is invisible. If there is a small thread running through all my work, it is that evil is never the other, everything is inside and never outside. – Claire Denis (in Jousse and Strauss 1994)

Claire Denis' film *Trouble Every Day* (2001) is a film as beautiful as it is brutal, an exploration of the interweaving of desire, hunger, sex, violence, bodies and borders. It is about the monster inside, unspeakable urges and the overwhelming need for complete incorporation. The film interrogates and crosses boundaries – between inside and outside, the familiar and the other, touch and penetration. Skin becomes a wound, a kiss turns into a bite and sex leads to cannibalism. *Trouble Every Day* caused a scandal at its premier at Cannes in 2001, and was, overall, not well-received, especially by US critics. It is certainly challenging but deserves to be reassessed for its thematic concerns, its surfeit of references and Denis' visceral aesthetic. Her sixth feature, *Trouble Every Day* followed the acclaim of *Beau Travail* (1999), her most widely-recognised and celebrated film. It was not the appealing eroticism Denis' audience expected to be roused by. *Trouble Every Day* is transgressive in its narrative and in its filmmaking. It is obsessed with the surface, with haptic images that pull the viewer into the distressing narrative, however uncomfortable – even painful – it is. Excessive violence is bound with vicious, all-consuming desire. The connection between physical and sexual hunger is one reason the film is disliked, with its turn to cannibalism inserting it to a tradition of offensive cinema, from the infamous exploitation of *Cannibal Holocaust* (Deodato, 1980) to the unfairly maligned *Neon Demon* (Refn, 2016). *Trouble Every Day* is part of a lineage of genre cinema that pushes the boundary of what can be shown on screen, aligned as much with Jacques Tourneau's *Cat People* (1942) as the New French Extremity. *Trouble Every Day* reflects the darkness of the world we live in, exploring desire, fantasy and autonomy in a compelling cinematic experience that beguiles and violates.

SYNOPSIS

Trouble Every Day follows the intersecting stories, and perhaps fates, of two couples: Léo (Alex Descas) and Coré (Beatrice Dalle) Semeneau and Shane (Vincent Gallo) and June (Tricia Vessey) Brown. Shane and June are American newlyweds visiting Paris on their honeymoon, a romantic sojourn that is actually a cover for Shane to find Léo. The men met previously on a research expedition into the South American jungle in search of a plant that would lead to a breakthrough in neurobiology, led by Léo and which Shane joined on behalf of a US pharmaceutical company. After publishing his unbelievable findings, Léo was shunned from the scientific community. Continuing his work in his own lab, he is compelled to discover a cure for the terrible condition that arose in human testing as his subject is, in fact, Coré. Her affliction presents as an uncontrollable and unquenchable hunger that leads her to seek out sex during which she consumes her partners. She escapes the house he keeps her locked up in, committing murders which he covers up. Shane, it seems, also contracted this disease, seeking out Léo in hope of answers as his condition deteriorates. He repeatedly leaves his new wife alone in the hotel, traveling through Paris alone under the guise of work. He visits the lab Léo used to run, meets with his former colleagues and wanders the city, plagued by insomnia which seems to fuel his growing lust. When he finally reaches the Semeneau house in the suburbs outside the city he finds Coré covered in blood, in a daze following her brutal murder of a teenage neighbour (which we witness). She is thrilled when Shane appears, but her embrace turns into another attack. After strangling her, he leaves the house to burn in a fire she had lit. He returns to the hotel where, overwhelmed by the same impulse as Coré, he tracks down the maid Christelle, resulting in an even more brutal murder. After showering, he tells June he is ready to go home, as she watches a single drop of blood streak down the shower curtain.

***

This linear description of the film is deceptive, contracting the elliptical and somewhat opaque plot. *Trouble Every Day* embodies Denis' statement 'I am trying to float on the impression of what a story could be' (in Romney 2000). The threads of the narrative come together slowly, with Denis making the viewer fill in the gaps, to decide on the details, with many questions suggested and then left unanswered. Did Shane and Coré both knowingly take part in unsanctioned human testing, trialling the drug themselves? Was Léo, as the leader of the team, aware of this experiment? Was Coré pressured into it or was it her idea? Was Shane's company pressuring him or did he do it for career progression? Did Shane take the drug himself or was he exposed by Coré – he denies having had an affair, but not fervently, so was this sexually transmitted? Why is Coré's affliction further progressed? Did the testing begin in Guyana, by ingesting the actual plant before it could be refined in the lab? Or was it safe in its natural state but dangerous when synthesised? Was the dose simply too high? How long ago was Guyana? Further viewings only produce more questions.

Alongside Coré and Shane's parallel stories, there is a second pair of characters who express a mutual interest with each of them. The teenager Erwan (Nicolas Duvauchelle), who lives across the road from Coré, is fascinated by her mysterious presence in the house and by Léo's strange behaviour. With her bedroom window across from his own, where he smokes cigarettes, bored by his life in the suburbs, Erwan looks to the house as a source of potential excitement. Christelle, the hotel maid, is also interested in Shane and June. The wealthy young American couple represent a different life than Christelle leads, enjoying the luxuries of the hotel that she provides. She is aware of Shane's intense gaze which is directed towards her. The last time she cleans the room, she lies on their bed and smokes one of their cigarettes, leaving an imprint of her body on the hotel bed, a reminder of her presence. Having watched her since he arrived, this is what finally pushes Shane to track her downstairs into the locker room and murder her. Neither of these victims realise the danger that they edge towards, how close they are to their deaths. It is an almost unconscious attraction, something imperceptible and instinctual, like how an animal lures its prey.

How *Trouble Every Day* developed

When production started on *Trouble Every Day*, Denis had been considering making a genre film for almost a decade. In 1991, she travelled to New York to shoot *Keep It for Yourself* (1991), a 40-minute black and white short commissioned by Nissan as one of three segments in *Figaro Stories* (along with Alejandro Agresti's *Library Love* and Kaizo Hayashi's *Man From The Moon*). This short was the first project of the American independent production and distribution company Good Machine, founded by Ted Hope and James Schamus (which became Focus Features). Schamus proposed to Denis that they make a horror feature together, as part of a series of six auteur-led films (Cindy Sherman's *Office Killer* of 1997 was the first). Denis explains in several interviews that she felt that, if she were to make a genre film, she had to approach it seriously, without pastiche or irony. Later, she and Olivier Assayas began working on a portmanteau film set in a hotel, centred on the idea of a foreign woman in Paris – they would each make one segment and Atom Egoyan a third. While this project never came to fruition, Assayas' concept was the genesis for *Irma Vep* (1996) and Denis' for *Trouble Every Day*. While waiting for approval to start making *Beau Travail* in Djibouti, she and her co-writer Jean-Pol Fargeau took her idea of a couple in a hotel room and created the script. Denis insists she had always imagined the man to be Gallo ('I would never have made this film without him') and the face of a woman at a window, who he was going to visit, had always been Dalle (in Bonnaud 2001). 'I knew they were like strange flowers both of them. Venomous,' she says (in *Dazed* 2011).

Denis describes a news story that was another decisive source for the plot of *Trouble Every Day*. 'One day I read this article that an American couple – working in a group of scientists, disappeared in the forests of New Guinea. Nobody found their bodies. It was so strange, like it was in the 19th century. I kept that in mind and little by little it grew. Like a scientific vampire story' (in *Dazed* 2011). The narrative for *Trouble Every Day* is also shaped by scientific research, which Denis detailed in an interview with Frédéric Bonnaud (2001). While writing the script, she and Fargeau read books by neurobiologist Jean-Pierre Changeux and also visited a lab to view the process of brain mapping. She read articles, noting a particular case from early-twentieth-century Wales where a brain injury apparently left a man with no sense of morality. Denis also mentions the business of medical research, with large American labs going to the Amazon and patenting plants with healing properties, which often have a ritual purpose for local communities. As much as science increasingly explains the world, Denis points to the fact that many are wary of it, craving the alternative medicine of plants in an almost primal way, a return to black magic: 'This vision of a reassuring science seemed to me no longer possible. The evil in question does not have a vaccine' (in Creutz 2001). The origin of the condition that Coré and Shane share lies somewhere between science and the supernatural, harnessing the dangerous power of nature to unlock the dangerous primal urges of humans. When *Trouble Every Day* was under development, alternative medicine was a topical subject. The use of herbal dietary supplements increased 380% between 1990 and 1997, during which time it was responsible for around $3.3 billion in sales in the United States (Eisenberg et al 1998). The market for alternative plant-based medicine has continued to grow: an estimated $46 billion was spent on dietary supplements in the United States in 2018 (cited in Khin et al 2020). Of course, there was also a popular interest in medical advancements in 2001. Specifically, Léo and Shane's search for a drug to affect the libido recalls the release of Viagra in 1998, which was a huge success, popularised by extensive interest from the media, and, quickly, in popular culture more widely.

CLAIRE DENIS BIOGRAPHY

Born in Paris in 1946, Denis spent most of her childhood in West Africa, where her father was a colonial official. They moved frequently, including to Cameroon, Somalia, Djibouti and Burkina Faso, though her parents taught her these places were not their home. However, for a long time, neither was France, and Denis expresses a feeling of being in-between, an outsider in both places. When she was twelve- or thirteen-years old, she and her sister contracted polio, returning to France where they were hospitalized – Denis recovered but her sister was paralysed. Beginning a new life in the suburbs of Paris, Denis enrolled in high school. Here, she joined the film club, which must have been a decisive moment in her life. Denis' love of cinema was established in childhood, stoked by her mother, who instead of telling her stories as a child, would describe films, such as Hitchcock's *The 39 Steps* (1935). She tells Aimé Ancian (2002) that in Africa they only had access to bad stocks of war films from America – her first memories of 'true' cinema were King Vidor's *War and Peace* (1956) and Satyajit Ray's *Pather Panchali* (1955). Denis began to visit Saint-Lazare Pasquier, an avant-garde cinema in Paris, where she discovered films by the directors who proved the most influential in her work, including Robert Bresson, Jean-Luc Godard, Michelangelo Antonioni and, later, Federico Fellini.

After high school, Denis studied economics (which she describes as 'completely suicidal') then, briefly, Oriental Languages. She married a photographer, who encouraged her to quit. After an internship with Télé Niger – a new educational television channel founded in 1964 – she joined the research department of the INA (Institut National de l'Audiovisuel). In 1969, Denis was accepted into IDHEC (L'Institut des hautes études cinématographiques – now La Fémis). 'I didn't at all think I would make films, it was a point in my life where I just told myself: here I am, let's take advantage of it,' she says (in Ancian 2002). After graduating in 1971 – by which time she seems to have been divorced – she worked as an assistant for directors such as Jacques Rivette on *Out 1* (1971), Denis Dusan Makavejev on *Sweet Movie* (1974) (her first paid role), Robert Enrico on *The Old Gun* (1974), Eduardo de Gregorio on *Sérail* (1976) and Costa-Gavras on *Hanna K.* (1983). After meeting Wim Wenders in Lisbon, Denis took up his invitation to travel to the United States to be his assistant director on *Paris, Texas* (1984). As they drove across the country, listening to Bob Dylan and the Pretenders, they developed the screenplay, an experience that shaped her approach to filmmaking. Agnès Godard, who has become Denis' most important collaborator, was the assistant to the cinematographer, Robbie Müller. On set, she met John Lurie, an actor, artist and musician, who had been part of the same No-Wave New York scene as Jim Jarmusch, Jean Michel Basquiat and Gallo (who was at one point his roommate). She followed him to New York, where she met Jarmusch – she believes that meeting these two men was the best thing to happen to her in the US. She even flew to New Orleans from Cameroon, where she was location scouting for her first film, *Chocolat*, to work on Jarmusch's *Down by Law* (1986) (using a different name to get around union regulations). Soon after, she travelled to Berlin for her final assistant director job on *Wings of Desire* (Wenders, 1987), where she again worked alongside Godard. Wenders recalls their late nights writing the script as they went, so spontaneous that they even created a new character after production had started. 'Claire was more than ready to make her own films. It would have been a waste to let her continue working as an assistant director,' he insists (in Vecchio 2014). Wenders helped her secure partial funding for *Chocolat* (he has a production credit) which she began filming later that year.

FILMOGRAPHY

Working on *Paris, Texas* and *Down by Law* helped Denis realise that she wanted to make her own films, to have more independence and ownership of her work. She wrote the screenplay for her first feature film, *Chocolat* (1988), a semi-autobiographical story about a French woman remembering her childhood in Cameroon, especially her relationship with the African man who is the family's servant. Realising she needed help with her draft, Denis collaborated with Jean-Pol Fargeau, establishing a co-writing partnership which continues today. *Chocolat* was incredibly well received, nominated for the Palme d'Or at Cannes. Her sophomore film, *Man No Run* (1989), following Les Têtes Brulées, a group of musicians from Cameroon, on tour in France, is the first of several documentaries she has made and a fairly unusual choice. Denis' next two narrative features delve into the underbelly of society: *No Fear, No Die – (S'en fout la mort)* (1990) is about the illegal cockfighting community and *I Can't Sleep (J'ai pas sommeil)* (1994) a serial killer who murders elderly women, based on a recent real-life case. *Nénette et Boni* (1996) explores the complicated relationship between an estranged brother and his unhappily pregnant sister. Denis' fifth, and arguably most lauded, film *Beau Travail* (1999) is about soldiers in the French Foreign Legion in Djibouti, a study of masculinity loosely based on Herman Melville's *Billy Budd* (1888). Following this acclaim, which stoked her international reputation, *Trouble Every Day* was undoubtedly a shock to much of Denis' audience, who anticipated something very different. Of Denis' next six films, five draw from existing texts and films. *Friday Night (Vendredi soir)* (2002), about two strangers who spend the night together, is an adaptation of Emmanuèle Bernheim's novel of the same name. The philosopher Jean Luc Nancy's short memoir about a heart transplant is the basis of *The Intruder (L'Intrus)* (2004). *35 Shots of Rum (35 rhums)* (2008) is inspired by Yasujirō Ozu's film *Banshun (Late Spring)* (1949) and *Bastards (Les Salauds)* (2013) by Akira Kurosawa's *The Bad Sleep Well (Warui yatsu hodo yoku nemuru)* (1960). The romantic comedy *Let the Sunshine In (Un beau soleil intérieur)* (2017) is inspired by Roland Barthes' *A Lover's Discourse: Fragments* (1977). In the centre of this list is *White Material* (2009), co-written by novelist Marie N'Diaye. A decade after *Beau Travail*, Denis returned to Cameroon to make this film about a white French woman in post-colonial Africa who remains on her family's coffee plantation despite the danger of rising civil conflict. Most recently, *High Life* (2018) is a sci-fi set on a prison spaceship.

Denis has made short films on a variety of subjects, including *Le 15 Mai* (1969) while studying at IDHEC, *Keep It for Yourself* (1991) and *Voilà l'enchaînement* (2014). She has also worked on anthologies such as *Pour Ushari Ahmed Mahmoud, Soudan* in *Lest We Forget (Contre l'oubli)* (1991), where Amnesty International commissioned thirty French filmmakers to make a plea on behalf of a political prisoner. *US Go Home* (1994) is a segment in *All the Boys and the Girls of Their Age (Tous les garçons et les filles de leur âge)*, a series of hour-long films commissioned by French television network Arte. *Nice, Very Nice* was a segment in *À propos de Nice, la suite* (1995) and *Towards Nancy (Vers Nancy)* in *Ten Minutes Older: The Cello* (2002). Denis' documentaries include *Jacques Rivette, le veilleur (Jacques Rivette, the Watchman)* (1990), *Towards Mathilde (Vers Mathilde)* (2005) and *Venezia 70 – Future Reloaded* (2013). In 2014, she filmed a short film *Contact*, named for the light installation by Danish artist Olafur Eliasson, which informed his work on the production design of *High Life*.

A central thread is in this diverse filmography is Denis' exploration of violence, desire, sex and, most palpably, the feeling of being an outsider. She repeatedly returns to the problem of belonging. The characters in her films reflect the experience of the other – whether a teenager, a serial killer, an immigrant or even someone unfamiliar with their own body. Physically and emotionally, they reside on the borders, grappling with who they are and how they fit into the world. These ideas are at the very core of *Trouble Every Day*.

APPROACH TO FILMMAKING

When asked why she chose to become a filmmaker, Denis declares 'I was absolutely unfit for anything else' (in Darke 2000). Her approach to filmmaking is highly collaborative, flexible and personal. When developing a film, Denis engages her team in continual conversations, spending time together to shape the narrative. Denis and Agnès Godard undertake extensive location scouting together, plotting out the visual geography of the film while, or even before, the script is written. While she plans everything out, Denis makes room for spontaneity on her shoots, an approach directly shaped by working with Wenders. According to Denis, he never complained when external forces, such as finances or weather, demanded he make changes, but took it as an opportunity to adapt the film: 'At that moment, the film itself becomes alive' (in Smith 2002). Her process is similarly dynamic. Denis does not do storyboards, feeling that everyone becomes dependent on them and so 'nothing interesting happens' (in Ross 2003). She also does not do shot descriptions. Godard finds this liberating to film 'something that is *being* written at that very moment…When you look at things for the very first time, you look at them with a particular sense of discovery and curiosity; you *dare* to look' (in Talu 2018). For similar reasons, Denis does not like rehearsing the script, anxious that the performances might be better before the camera is on, so she and Fargeau write scenes just for rehearsal purposes. Yet, the screenplay itself is not fixed: 'I don't at all like the idea of a screenplay being a cage and that inside the cage you have to direct the actors. It seems to me that a screenplay is a kind of take-off' (in Sotinel 2001).

Denis' decade of experience working with other directors helped her learn to trust the filmmaking process. She tells Damon Smith (2002): 'What I got from Jacques Rivette was a complete trust in filmmaking, in actors, in acting…and a taste for endangering myself a little bit…From Wim [Wenders], I got another kind of trust, a trust in feeling very free with the camera and in designing a film not with an aesthetic, but with a complete trust of a location, in the light of the day.' Denis offers the people she works with a similar freedom, encouraging them to be part of the process, including her actors. For instance, she reveals that in *Trouble Every Day*, the scenario for the two on-screen murder scenes stopped at the bite and the actors led from there: 'They almost took control of the movie!' (in Creutz 2001). She envisions this autonomy as something very physical: 'In a way, I see it more like choreography. This is to say that for me, directing is something that goes through the body. Directing and acting exist in an organic relation similar to a dance' (in Reid 1996). Godard similarly considers herself a dancer, of sorts, filming with her entire body. She describes finding her rhythm as a cinematographer within the actors' rhythm, where she is not only a witness to a scene but brings it to life.

THE TEAM

Denis has a small group of people with whom she has worked repeatedly throughout her career, developing close relationships based on trust and a shared vision. This familiarity allows her the flexibility that she aims for while filming ('if filming means you have to control everything, I'd shoot myself' – Sotinel 2001). A cohort of these regular collaborators worked on *Trouble Every Day*. Denis wrote the script with Fargeau, her co-writer on ten screenplays, including all five features before it. Nelly Quettier is the editor on *I Can't Sleep* and *Beau Travail*, and later *Vendredi soir* and *The Intruder*. Costume designer Judy Shrewsbury has worked on every Denis feature over the last twenty years, from *Beau Travail* to *High Life*. Arnaud de Moleron is the production designer for *I Can't Sleep*, *Nénette et Boni*, *Beau Travail*, *The Intruder*, *35 Shots of Rum*, and *Let the Sunshine In*. Jean-Louis Ughetto is a sound designer in *Chocolat*, *I Can't Sleep*, *Nénette et Boni*, *Vendredi soir* and *The Intruder*. The soundtrack for *Trouble Every Day* is by English band Tindersticks, led by Stuart Staples. They are the composers on eight of Denis' films: *Nénette et Boni*, *35 Shots of Rum*, *Bastards*, *White Material*, *The Intruder*, *Let the Sunshine In*, and *High Life*. Denis met the band backstage after a show at the Bataclan in Paris in 1995. She had been listening to their music while writing *Nénette et Boni* and, after asking to use their song 'My Sister', the band offered to write the soundtrack. Since their first collaboration, Denis has worked repeatedly with the band, and sometimes just Staples, the lead singer and guitarist. She believes the musician 'has a rapport with the body, with flesh, with desire which is very close to mine' (in Ancian 2002). This shared vision is obviously important in *Trouble Every Day*. 'Fundamentally what we do with Claire is create an emotional response to her images', Staples explains (in Anderson 2002). However, the music also in turn inspires Denis, shaping her work.

Agnès Godard is perhaps Denis's most important collaborator. The cinematographer has worked on eleven of Denis' features, starting out as a camera operator on *Chocolat* and *No Fear, No Die*, before serving as the cinematographer in every film except *White Material* and *High Life*. Denis and Godard both attended IDHEC, though they graduated several years apart. Their first film together was the aforementioned *Paris, Texas*. Godard had previously filmed Wim Wenders' *Chambre 666* (1982) – her first job as a cinematographer – and *The State of Things* (1982). She has worked with many celebrated directors, including Peter Greenaway (*A Zed & Two Noughts*, 1985), Agnès Varda (*Jacquot de Nantes*, 1991) and Michelangelo Antonioni (*Beyond the Clouds*, 1995). Denis and Godard's close relationship was cemented during the difficult shoot for *Chocolat*. Denis describes it as 'very idealistic. When you nourish one another it can work, but it's like being in a couple' (in Darke 2000). The women have developed a style that builds images and spaces, not so much translating the world onto the screen but building the narrative world. Denis explains 'we do not ask ourselves visual questions but rather questions of space' (in Harrer 2001b). When detailing the process of working with Denis, Godard says 'curiously with Claire, I have a hard time speaking of shots, and I rather speak in terms of images… she has images in mind, and sometimes it's enough to have a few images and trust that they will add up to each other to create an inventory' (in Talu 2018).

Denis also repeatedly returns to certain actors, with whom she develops close relationships. 'I work again and again with the same actors and actresses because… otherwise I'm missing them…I choose their clothes, I choose the way they speak, they're like mine and I hate when they work on other films...Beatrice Dalle, Vincent Gallo, both of them, they are mine' (in Hynes 2012). She had formerly worked with most of the cast of *Trouble Every Day*. Denis met Gallo in New York in the 1990s; after he was cast in *Keep It for Yourself*, she decided to write a film tailored to his screen presence. He later travelled to France to film *US Go Home* and also Denis' next feature, *Nénette et Boni*, where he played Vincenzo Brown (the same surname from *Trouble Every Day* and his own 1998 film, *Buffalo 66*). After appearing in these two films with Gallo, Alice Houri then appeared alongside him in a brief scene in *Trouble Every Day*. Dalle's first role with Denis, in *I Can't Sleep*, was by happenstance. The women had met through Jarmusch while Dalle was filming *Night on Earth* (1992). When the actor who was to play Mona pulled out of Denis' film just weeks before filming commenced, Dalle offered to do it. She then accepted a role in *The Intruder*, which also features Florence Loiret Caille, Christelle in *Trouble Every Day*, who returned to work with Denis again in *Bastards*. Alex Descas appears in eight of Denis' features over a period of two decades, starting with *Nénette et Boni*, followed by *I Can't Sleep*, *The Intruder*, *35 Shots of Rum*, *Bastards*, and *Let the Sunshine In*. Nicolas Duvauchelle plays a legionnaire in *Beau Travail* and later appears in *White Material* and *Let the Sunshine In*. *Trouble Every Day* is the only time Denis worked with American actor Tricia Vessey, who she cast after seeing her in an early cut of Jarmusch's *Ghost Dog: The Way of the Samurai* (1999).

With Dalle and Gallo cast as the leads, *Trouble Every Day* was always going to be controversial. Both are recognised for their roles in independent cinema. They had both recently been in films directed by Abel Ferrara – Gallo in *The Funeral* (1996) and Dalle in *The Blackout* (1997). But, they are more notorious for their controversial personal lives and openly expressing their unfiltered, often provocative, opinions. Their reputations are difficult to extricate from the reception of the film. In a review for *The Guardian*, Peter Bradshaw (2002) proposes that *Trouble Every Day* needed 'actors less absurdly and outrageously conceited than Béatrice Dalle and Vincent Gallo'.

Dalle has openly discussed her tumultuous personal life. After leaving home age fifteen to live in Paris, she lived as a squatter and shoplifted frequently (from designers such as Dior, Yves Saint Laurent and Jean Paul Gaultier). She has been arrested several times, for assault and drug possession, which in 1997 led to a seven year ban from the US (slapping an American embassy official could not have helped her case). Dalle had relationships with Rupert Everett and Joey Starr before meeting her second husband, Guenaël Meziani, while he was serving a twelve year sentence at the Centre Pénitentiaire de Ploemeur in Brittany. She was there researching a role in *Tête d'or* (2006) – they married in the prison and divorced soon after his release. Dalle's outspoken opinions range from the blithe ('I still prefer to eat a Bounty than to have a child') to the inappropriate – claiming on television that she met Julien Maury, co-director of *À l'intérieur* (2007), 'in the chatroom on a farm-sex website'. In a completely baffling interview on 'Le Divan with Marc-Olivier Fogiel' on France 3, which aired in February 2016, she casually admitted to having actually tasted human flesh (a revelation that, several years earlier, would surely have helped garner more coverage for *Trouble Every Day*). As she tells it, after taking acid, she and her friends cut off the ear of a man at a morgue and tasted it, noting that he did not complain. As this was fifteen years after *Trouble Every Day*, it was not a press gimmick, though, unsurprisingly, it was picked up by several news outlets. Denis believes that behind Dalle's scandalous declarations, 'she loves to work, she likes and defends the films she makes' (in Ancian 2002).

Dalle's public image was established by her first role in Jean-Jacques Beineix's *Betty Blue* (*37°2 le matin*) (1986). As the titular Betty, she portrays a passionate, unstable and violent young woman whose mental health disintegrates. The film was an international success, receiving several award nominations, including for Best Foreign Language Film at the 1987 Oscars. With its nudity and explicit sex scenes, Dalle was immediately established as a sex symbol, a reputation that is drawn from in *Trouble Every Day*, although William Thomas (2002) says Coré 'will have anyone who once possessed that ubiquitous *Betty Blue* poster finally erasing any erotic fantasies'. Many reviews of Dalle's performance as Coré are openly sexualised – for instance, Derek Elley (2002) writes 'As the camera roams over her naked body, one portion of her anatomy literally looks good enough to eat'. Bradshaw (2002) describes Coré as 'a cross between Sylvia Kristel and Hannibal Lecter' (Kristel's most famous role is as Emmaunelle in the 1970s-1980s soft-core exploitation series of the same name). Dalle's nickname is 'La Grande Bouche' (The Big Mouth) – Philip French (2002) even, bewilderingly, comments in his review of *Trouble Every Day* that 'blood drips from her mouth, which is one of the three largest in the cinema today (the others belong to Julia Roberts and Sandra Bernhard)'. Dalle reached a different, much broader, audience in the horror film *À l'intérieur* (2007), where, coincidentally, she murders Duvauchelle on screen a second time.

Gallo's career has taken several paths; aside from acting, writing, producing and directing films, he has worked as an artist, musician, model, motorcycle racer, trader of hi-fi goods and also made shrewd investments in real estate by renowned architects (most recently a compound in Tucson designed by Rick Joy). When asked which he was the best at, he answers 'Counting money. I can count 10,000 dollars in one dollar bills in 32 seconds. That's a record. I'm the greatest cash counter that ever lived' (in Sanders 1997). After what he describes as a complex childhood, including an abusive parent and engaging in illegal activities ('in crime I showed my best talent…I could steal a car better than anyone I've ever known in my life' – in Takano 2004), Gallo moved to New York. He became a well-known figure in the No Wave community of the late-1970s, attested to in his appearance in the infamous documentary *Downtown 81* (Edo Bertoglio, 1981). Gallo played bass in the experimental noise band Gray with his friend, artist Jean-Michel Basquiat. He was also a practicing artist, holding his first solo exhibition at Annina Nosei's gallery on Prince Street in 1985: 'The end-of-the-world feeling Gallo's pictures transmit is peculiarly calming,' Gary Indiana wrote in his *Village Voice* review (Indiana 2018). He appeared alongside Kate Moss in Calvin Klein's 1995 campaign. Gallo was reportedly engaged to Asia Argento in 1998, though he later refuted this. Throughout the 1990s, Gallo was cast in high-profile films such as *Goodfellas* (Scorsese, 1990) with Robert De Niro and Joe Pesci, *Arizona Dream* (Kusturica, 1993) with Johnny Depp and Fay Dunaway, and *The House of the Spirits* (August, 1993) with Meryl Streep, Winona

Ryder, Jeremy Irons, Antonio Banderas, Glenn Close and Vanessa Redgrave. He also directed his first feature-length film, *Buffalo 66*, which he also wrote, starred in and composed the music for. Billy Brown (Gallo), recently released from prison for a crime he did not commit, kidnaps a tap dancer (Christina Ricci) and forces her to pretend to be his wife for his parents (Anjelica Houston and Ben Gazzara). It was a financial and critical success. The response to his sophomore film *Brown Bunny* (2003) was the opposite. Following an infamous Cannes debut – met with boos and even singing from Roger Ebert, it was variously described as boring, bold, self-indulgent and pornographic (its most widely discussed scene was Chloe Sevigny performing unsimulated fellatio on Gallo).

Gallo's public personality may have influenced assessments of his role in *Trouble Every Day*, which many critics disliked. He certainly seems to cultivate this response – his interviews are rife with sexist, racist, homophobic and anti-Semitic comments. On his website, Gallo sells his sexual services and even his sperm. He also would not generate much support after his criticism of individuals in the industry. In one interview of 2004, he commented 'Steven Soderbergh sucks…Wes Anderson sucks. Spike Jonze sucks bad. James Gray sucks… Sofia Coppola is a parasite' (in Takano 2014). Criticism of Gallo in *Trouble Every Day* is closely tied to his appearance. 'Ratty-looking and pasty-skinned with a high-pitched voice, the actor is closer to a neuresthenic Charles Manson than a magnetic homme fatal', writes Stephen Holden in *The New York Times* (2002). Resembling 'a Nixon-era drug dealer, the very picture of depravity' (O'Hehir 2002), Gallo is felt to be so creepy 'that even in the scene where he gets out of the shower he looks as if he could use a shower' (LaSalle 2002). French (2002) insists that 'Gallo, with his Rasputin stare and ill-tended beard, is the kind of doctor who, if he was known to make house calls in your neighbourhood, would have everyone rushing out to buy extra locks and chains'.

RECEPTION

The critical response to *Trouble Every Day* was predominantly negative, especially in the US. It is widely considered unusual – even a misstep – in Denis' oeuvre. The film premiered out of competition at Cannes in 2001, screening at midnight on 13 May. It was apparently met by booing and two women in the audience fainted, making it one of those infamous screenings in cinema history where an ambulance had to be called. On hearing this news, Denis said 'I thought I was going to pass out myself on the spot but the person who told me this said, "No, on the contrary, this is very good"' (in B. de M. 2001). Of course, this incident fuelled the interest of the press – Thomas Sotinel even dedicated his review in Le Monde to these two women, a choice that played into the hype around the shockingly gruesome scenes. Denis, however, feels that it is 'weird to measure a film by how much scandal it makes or how much violence it contains; it feels like you're manipulating the audience. I think it is a very naive and innocent film, but in the end it is what it is: either people like it or they don't' (in Smith 2002).

The reception at Cannes situates Trouble Every Day into a tradition of un- and under-appreciated debuts at the festival. Films by esteemed directors which were booed include Michelangelo Antonioni's L'Avventura (1960), Carl Theodor Dreyer's Gertrud (1964), Martin Scorsese's Taxi Driver (1976), Jane Campion's Sweetie (1989), David Lynch's Wild at Heart (1990) and David Cronenberg's Crash (1997). The walkouts due to Trouble Every Day's graphic violence closely align the film with other Cannes premieres such Gaspar Noe's Irréversible in 2002 and Lars Von Trier's Antichrist in 2009. The response at Cannes established Trouble Every Day as a film maudit – which translates to 'cursed film' – a category of maligned, taboo-breaking cinema. However, it was awarded the 17th Prix Très Spécial, an annual award founded in 1985 by Gérard Lenne and Jean-Claude Romer (and abandoned in 2006) in recognition of films that show imagination, disrespect, insolence, even bad taste. Both men are critics with a shared interest in the fantastic who served on selection committees, including for the Avoriaz Fantastic Film Festival. The range of international films awarded this prize include the Austrian Funny Games (Haneke, 1997), Mexican-Italian Santa Sangre (Jodorowsky, 1989), Australian Bad Boy Bubby (de Heer, 1993), New Zealand Meet the Feebles (Jackson, 1989), Spanish Anguish (Luna, 1987) and North American The Devil's Rejects (Zombie, 2005). Lucile Hadzihalilovic and Noé (who are, coincidentally, married) are the only two directors who won twice, for La Bouche de Jean-Pierre (1996) and Innocence (2004) and Carne (1991) and I Stand Alone (1998), respectively. The award emphasises that films which might not be appreciated by the general public, like Trouble Every Day, have supporters who recognise them as special. Many of the winners have since gained more interest as a result and even become cult favourites.

Trouble Every Day opened in French cinemas on 11 July 2001. Over the next two years, it screened across the world, primarily at film festivals, including: Toronto in September 2001 and Stiges in October, Rotterdam in January 2002, Finland in September 2002 and Melbourne in August 2003. The film had a limited US release on 30 November 2001 and later screened in New York at Quad Cinema on 1 March 2002. The UK premiere was not until 27 December 2002. English-language reviews were largely negative, which is reflected in review aggregator sites. As of January 2021, *Trouble Every Day* is Denis's lowest rated film on Metacritic and Rotten Tomatoes and second lowest on IMDb (0.2 points below *High Life*). As with many films, both foreign and horror, limited theatrical release meant that viewers often had to wait for DVDs, with availability differing depending on distributors and regions. Access was further restricted as it did not receive a rating from the MPAA, a further limitation for distribution both in cinemas and home video stores. This would have shaped the slow reassessment of the film which is reflected in the slight changes in average ratings, with an overall increase. User reviews on IMDb rose from 5.6/10 in June 2004 to 6/10 January 2021. For critic reviews, the ranking on Rotten Tomatoes increased from 48% in September 2004 to 50% in January 2021 (with a drop to 44% in the middle) and on Metacritic, from 36% in January 2012 to 40% January 2021. Of course, these ratings are still very low and *Trouble Every Day* is, overall, still Denis' least liked film. However, results are slightly different on French aggregator AlloCiné. The average viewer rating is similarly low, at 2.5 stars, but for critics it is 4.2, a significant difference which supports the general impression that French critics were impressed by the film and, perhaps, were the most familiar with what Denis was attempting.

Several thoughtful and favourable reviews of *Trouble Every Day* were published in France in 2001. For instance, Jean-Pierre Dufreigne deemed it 'beautiful' and 'elegant' and Jean-Marc Lalanne claimed that 'this incandescent sense of poetry and staging make Claire Denis a unique filmmaker'. Louis Guichard described the film as 'bathed in an exhilarating decoction of sensuality and mystery, melancholy and fatality'. In *Le Monde*, Sotinel suggested that the 'excruciating pain that runs through *Trouble Every Day* might be unbearable if it did not give the screen a rare, almost serene beauty'. Elysabeth François felt that the experience of horror is 'transcended by sublime plastic effects combining sensuality of the epidermis (skin) and ferocity of wounds'. For Bonnaud, the film 'is more than a splendid formal object. It is an act of faith.' Nancy, who has an ongoing collaborative dialogue with Denis, wrote 'Icône de l'archarnement', a long article exploring the film as an important cultural object, for the film journal *Trafic*.

Outside of France, the reviews for *Trouble Every Day* were overwhelmingly negative, with some especially vicious criticism published in the US press on its release in 2002. Writing for *Variety*, Derek Elley deems it 'resolutely silly… Over-long, under-written and needlessly obscure.' Mick LaSalle is even more negative in the *San Francisco Gate*, branding it 'an artistic flop, torpedoed by an idiotic premise and by Denis' turgid approach to the story'. In the *Austin Chronicle*, Marjorie Baumgarten insists 'any fainting among viewers of *Trouble Every Day* is more likely to derive from boredom rather than the sight of horror'. Andrew O'Hehir likens watching it to 'biting into what looks like a juicy, delicious plum on a hot summer day and coming away with your mouth full of rotten pulp and living worms', a visceral description in *Salon*. In *The Observer*, Philip French considers it 'a risible disaster… confused, incoherent' and in *The Guardian*, Peter Bradshaw considers it 'very silly indeed'. Holden sums it up in the *New York Times* as a 'daring, intermittently beautiful failure of a movie'.

Such negative, even derisive, assessments of *Trouble Every Day* have slowly shifted in the almost two decades since it was released. However, it is still felt by many to be a blip in Denis' filmography. In an interview of 2010 Andrew Hussey positions *Trouble Every Day* as a 'disastrous error…Its ludicrous plot about sex-hungry cannibalistic vampires in Paris drew derisive laughter when it was screened in Cannes and its gory scenes had even hardened horror fans retching in disgust.' If it had been made today, it might have had a very different reception. Amid a heightened interest in representations of women on screen and persistent debates about 'prestige horror' and 'post-horror' (which assume horror has just recently become about something, missing the point entirely), there might have been more interest in the film. There are certainly now more platforms for promoting and discussing the film. At the very least, it surely would have found its audience more quickly and easily with the ease of access through digital streaming compared to being when rolled out in limited release over a number of years.

WHY *TROUBLE EVERY DAY*?

Trouble Every Day is an immensely difficult film to watch. So, why do it? What do viewers get out of it? Considering the film in terms of genre, style and references, this book seeks to reposition *Trouble Every Day* as a multifaceted text that is more than its shocking reputation. As a critical study, it leans heavily on close visual analysis that prioritises images, drawing from art history. This is apparent in chapter 2, 'An Inventory of Images', a detailed breakdown of the film that serves as a counter-argument to reproaches that it is boring, incoherent and shallow, with no discernible plot. The chapter delves into the narrative and stylistic choices being made in each scene as they are woven together into an elliptical plot, uncovering layers of meaning. This continues in chapter 3, 'Borders/Bodies', which explores the intersections between screen, surface, touch, gaze and desire. *Trouble Every Day* narratively and formally interrogates the idea of the boundary, including spatial constructions like windows, the fragile division between public and private spaces and the skin as a corporeal frontier. Drawing from a range of theories, including phenomenology, haptic images and abjection, this chapter includes formal analysis of the film, including sound design. It also considers its creation of images and sensations through the lens of art history, drawing comparison to the Baroque and the Rococo. The fourth chapter, 'Situating the Film', examines many of the references within *Trouble Every Day*, not only from cinema but also art, photography, literature and folklore. Though it is often assessed in terms of its place in the New French Extremity movement, the film is part of a long lineage of boundary-pushing cinema. There are nods to various genres and time periods, including mad science, video nasties, Italo-exploitation, the Gothic and Golden Age Hollywood horror. As the references expand – the tale of Beauty and the Beast, Jeff Wall's photography and Abstract Expressionism – it becomes increasingly difficult to situate the film. The final chapter briefly considers *Trouble Every Day*'s legacy, including its ever-evolving influence and modes of reception as well as Denis' career. As the film has discovered new audiences over the past two decades, there has been a shift away from the initial negative responses. *Trouble Every Day* is of interest not despite but because of its polarising nature. The things it is criticised for – unclear plot, unlikable characters, unidentified nature of Coré and Shane's condition – are part of what makes it so intriguing, allowing viewers to discover and imagine meaning.

2. An Inventory of Images: Assembling an Elliptical Narrative

Trouble Every Day is a film defined by its images, where meaning is drawn out rather than presented, fluid rather than prescribed. By approaching its progression scene-by-scene, this chapter emphasises the deliberate choices that Denis makes along with her team. This detailed breakdown delves into both narrative and stylistic aspects of the film, exploring the layers of meaning that can be unwound. In this way, it counters claims repeated in many audience reviews, where detractors describe the film as boring, with a thin plot where 'nothing happens'. These responses are telling, reflecting the difficult nature of the film, where much happens below the surface. However, examining the scenes one by one reveals that more is happening than might be immediately apparent. While the vague and elliptical plot might cause confusion, there are hints and suggestions. For instance, sounds overlap across scenes and the music composed by Tindersticks unifies the soundtrack. The use of red stands out in the grey of winter, where Paris is drained of colour. A plethora of visual references are evoked, such as Gallo playing as Quasimodo atop Notre Dame, Dalle as a damsel in distress locked up in her room, Degas' women bathing, and Danny's tricycle in *The Shining* (Kubrick, 1981). These references are explored further in chapter 4. This chapter demonstrates that *Trouble Every Day* rewards close analysis and repeated viewings.

Opening

Trouble Every Day opens with an abstract introduction of the idea at the very centre of the film – unquenchable desire, and how the kiss can become a bite. Shot in almost complete darkness, the camera sits just outside the window of a parked car where a man and woman are kissing. It lingers close to the couple for close to a minute, an uncomfortably long period. Moving down her neck several times, it hints at a danger which, ultimately, does not play out. He leans over her, fingers stroking her neck, a sensual gesture that teases he might strangle her. In the opening of a horror film, this couple would meet an untimely death, but here the screen fades to black for 25 seconds – an interminably long time – leaving the viewer to focus on the haunting theme song by

Tindersticks, which plays throughout the scene. Denis felt this song was so important that she rearranged the whole screenplay in response to it, insisting it had to be at the start (Ancian 2002). The original opening scene was actually of the plane, with this kissing scene planned for later as Shane walked through Paris. Forgoing a more logical structure, this adjustment immediately establishes the elliptical nature of the plot. The couple in the car are divorced from the narrative, existing solely to embody the connection between desire and danger. For Denis, the subject is not the couple but the kiss itself: 'all the film is there. Inside a kiss between two lovers, anything is possible, including the worst violence' (in Gonzales 2001). The black screen finally reveals lights reflected on the Seine at night, shimmering in the gentle waves, the sound of running water immersing the viewer in the romance of the scene. The focus progressively widens to show more as the sky lightens – bridges, banks, pink-hued dawn – orienting the viewer in space.

Coré and Léo

In the pale light of dusk, Coré stands beside a van parked next to a graffitied building. Pulling on a coat which seems much too large over a black slip and knee-high boots, she appears cold and vulnerable, an impression disturbed by her oddly coy behaviour. A passing truck slows, its driver staring at Coré, before reversing. As the man walks towards her, the camera cuts twice to a close-up of her seductive, almost sly, expression (Fig. 1). The camera turns to the unattractive setting of telegraph posts and utilitarian building blocks. Léo arrives on his motorbike after nightfall. Discovering the truck, the still-ajar door reveals the key in the ignition, a familiar trope. He also finds the van empty. In an eerie wide shot of overgrown dry yellowed grass, viewed from behind a group of bare trees, Léo emerges from the black background (Fig. 2). The tall grass rustles in the breeze and a low industrial hum overlay a series of shots of the vacant land, one revealing a body. We follow Léo's feet to the man, half-naked, who he turns over to reveal a gruesome mutilated face. Nearby, almost obscured by the rushes, sits Coré, arms wrapped around her knees, audibly chewing. Walking up behind her, Léo unexpectedly gently rubs her back, kisses her face and pulls her back towards him, stroking her blood covered face. Free of dialogue, this interaction establishes a non-verbal communication between the couple which continues throughout the film.

Figs. 1 & 2

This scene subverts conventions and expectations, not just from the horror genre but a wider range of thriller, drama and crime texts. Coré is set up as a traditional victim – a woman, alone, on the side of the road who approaches a passing driver, presumably in need of assistance. Yet, it is his body found lying in a field. Unlike women victims on screen, whose faces are usually untouched to maintain their appearance, this man's disfigured face renders him almost unrecognisable. Coré joins a tradition of murderous women on film, an unusual, though not unheard of, narrative. The fierce wounds inflicted on this man imply a surprising ferocity and strength. Reviewers such as Bonnaud, Dufreigne and Isabelle Danel compare Coré to a jungle cat and this field to a savannah, tying *Trouble Every Day* into Denis' earlier films set in Africa. There is certainly something cat-like about Coré, yet she is not a shapeshifter but a very real person. The alternate story here, one which would be much more familiar to viewers, would be the authorities searching for missing people, a hunt for a serial killer disposing of bodies but leaving behind crime scenes on the outskirts of the city. But there is no reference to that possible narrative here.

JUNE AND SHANE

The exterior of a plane window frames the faces of June and Shane, who peer out at the world below (Fig. 3). When she says something that makes him smile he kisses her cheek and she smiles back – a mirror to the previous scene of tenderness between Léo and Coré. The rumbling noise of the plane obscures their interchange, so Gallo has the first line of dialogue, seven and a half minutes into the film. 'I think those lights are Denver', he says, over an aerial shot of a grid of city lights. Champagne flute in hand, he toasts 'To Mr and Mrs Brown'. He asks his bride 'I'm happy. Are you happy? I'm happy', seeming hesitant, repeating the word happy as if it will make it true. Staring at the inside of her wrist in a distinctly vampiric way, he kisses along the inside of her arm.

Fig. 3

As the passengers sleep, Shane crouches in the bathroom, arms around knees like Coré, overwhelmed by a disjointed, blood-soaked fantasy. An image of a hand covered in blood is followed by a sequence of images of June naked, covered in a sheet drenched in blood, palpably heavy with the dense liquid the fabric cannot contain (Fig. 4). The effect is a cross between a giallo nightmare and the wet drapery technique in classical sculpture. The camera glides across her body, lingering on fragmented body parts, like her face, arm and neck. It settles on a close-up of her eyes which blink and then close – is she dead or simply sated? Will she be Shane's victim? Or will she join him in his compulsion, which might even be contagious? Shane is shaken from his dark reverie by a flight attendant knocking on the door. Back in his seat, June lies across him and he pulls the blanket over her, rubs her back and kisses the top of head. Though he is affectionate and protective, he must know he is the danger. Opening the shade, the sun streams in, a moment that Denis says in the DVD audio commentary is significant, where he is eaten by the light. The sunshine might hold the monster inside at bay for a time but it does not kill him, like a vampire, because, like Coré, he is all too corporeal.

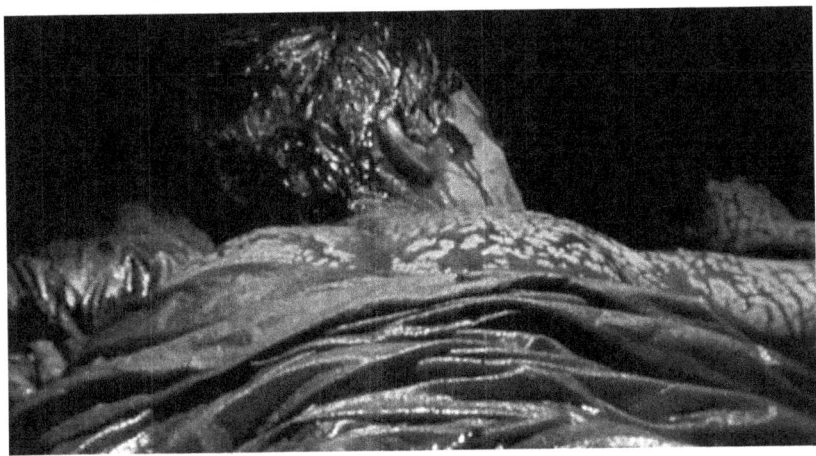

Fig. 4

THE SUBURBS

A series of shots show a Paris suburb, including a plane flying overhead. The movement of these passengers – including June and Shane, who we could imagine to be arriving on that very plane – contrast to Coré's literal captivity and Erwan's metaphorical confinement. The teenager is introduced looking out his bedroom window, bored of his suburban life. Across the street, Léo closes the shutters on Coré's bedroom, fastening a heavy bar before locking the windows, a gothic trope, though here we should not support the typical heroine's goal of escape. Wearing just a gown and with wet hair – following a bathing ritual we will see later – Coré hugs Léo. They kiss and, as he pulls her down onto the bed, she giggles. This is their most relaxed and human interaction throughout the film, an echo of their past relationship. The moment is disrupted by Léo swiftly pulling away – Coré is too hungry and he knows what will happen next. He leaves, locking the door behind him. Coré angrily discards the pills he left her, another trope, though it is unclear what is causing her murderous behaviour – perhaps it is him? Again, this scene is free of dialogue, suggesting the couple have such a long history that they do not need words or maybe, more bleakly, they have nothing left to say.

Erwan watches Léo leave on his motorcycle. In an exterior shot, a second teen joins him at the window. At the Semenaus' fence, Erwan urges 'come on' before climbing over into the yard. This is the first dialogue in five minutes and, at the fifteen minute mark, barely thirty words have been spoken. Coré lounges on her bed, still wearing her silky purple robe, very much the stereotype of a seductress. Lifting a lamp, she uncovers a hidden key with which she opens the window only to discover the shutters locked. From below, the teens see these shake as she furiously tries to release them, a sound likened by Denis in the audio commentary to a caged beast. The incident leaves Erwan equally scared and intrigued. Léo, it is revealed, is a doctor, treating patients as a general physician, which is later revealed to be very different work to his previously successful career in medical research. This is the first of just two scenes where he has dialogue in the film, and his only present-day conversation, so it is frustrating that the brief exchange is only him talking to a patient. Meanwhile, Coré reveals another hidden item – an electric saw she has improbably managed to stow under the bed. We see her looking out through a small, high window with bars on it, built into the old stone wall (Fig. 5). She strokes the glass with her fingers, a tactile action that engages the haptic gaze. This image of the woman at the window is another trope, one that informs the entire film (discussed in more detail in chapter 3). Denis says that as she wrote the script, this face had always been Dalle's (in Bonnaud 2001).

Fig. 5

THE HOTEL

Shane and June arrive at their hotel. From inside the car, June turns to watch Shane helping the woman unload their luggage, smiling; from her point of view we see him smile briefly back at her. The camera swoops up and across the Parisian street, quickly taking in the architecture and the bare trees, capturing June's disorientation in this new place. From inside the hotel, we see her standing still as she looks around slowly, impeccably dressed in a powder blue wool coat with Peter Pan collar, pearl earrings and white gloves, handbag and shoes. She looks decisively old-fashioned, evoking Audrey Hepburn with her dark pixie cut and large eyes. Compared to Coré in the previous scene, June appears especially proper and innocent. Has she dressed up for the trip, trying to live out a fantasy of the Parisian honeymoon gleaned from mid-century films? Or is this who she is at home? It is easy to imagine this image of June standing alone outside the hotel, a woman in foreign city, appearing in the original concept for the portmanteau film. Again evoking the gothic narrative, June is the young ingénue left alone to discover the truth about whatever dark happenings she is about to face, unsurprisingly tied to her new husband. In an extreme close-up, Shane rubs his eyes and temples – is it jetlag, or a symptom of whatever is giving him these visions? Reminiscent of The Shining, when Jack opens his eyes and Lloyd appears behind the bar, Shane sees the uniformed man awaiting behind the front desk. His disembodied voice says 'I'm Mr Brown' as the camera reveals June still outside looking around, not joining him until the end of the men's exchange. When Shane asks for help with luggage, the man calls Christelle.

CHRISTELLE

Christelle is introduced with a shot of her bare calves beneath a striped uniform, dragging the luggage ahead of the couple, before the camera moves up to the back of her head. She glances back, twice, and Shane stares at her, his gaze lingering at the nape of her neck, evoking a very different scene from a horror movie, of a woman being followed down a dark street. Shane carries June over the threshold, they kiss, and he sits with her in his lap on the unmade bed, which Christelle is awkwardly still attempting to make. When Shane lies down, pulling June on top of him, she gets up to help Christelle, behaviour which is presumably just as uncomfortable for the maid. He runs his hands along the edge of the clean white linen, reminding of his dream of June wrapped in the blood-soaked sheet. The camera reveals his penetrative stare, before panning across to show Christelle is still the object of his gaze. She is seen in profile from his point of view – hair loosely pulled back, lilac eyeshadow and gaze pointedly averted.

The camera tracks the back of Christelle's neck as she wheels her cart back down the hall, the close-up preventing an orientation of the geography of the hotel (Fig. 6). She swipes a few tiny jam jars off a cart she passes, a minor act of rebellion, a way to experience a small part of the luxury her work provides for others. Downstairs in the service area, hidden from the view of guests, she moves towards us along a brightly lit tiled hallway, where, away from the carpet, the wheels click rhythmically. The utilitarian space, with its old service elevator, pallets, chipped paint and fluorescent lighting, contrasts to the grandeur upstairs; it exists solely to make the hotel function. The location is a double, much like Christelle is for June, the loose-fitting plain uniform contrasting with the tailored, expensive-looking suit. This upstairs/downstairs comparison again brings to mind *The Shining*, where the Torrances are the temporary custodians of the Overlook Hotel, living in the staff area to ensure its grandeur is maintained for the next season. For guests, the hermetic world of the hotel feels comfortable, immaculate and secure, an illusion fashioned by the work that goes on behind the scenes.

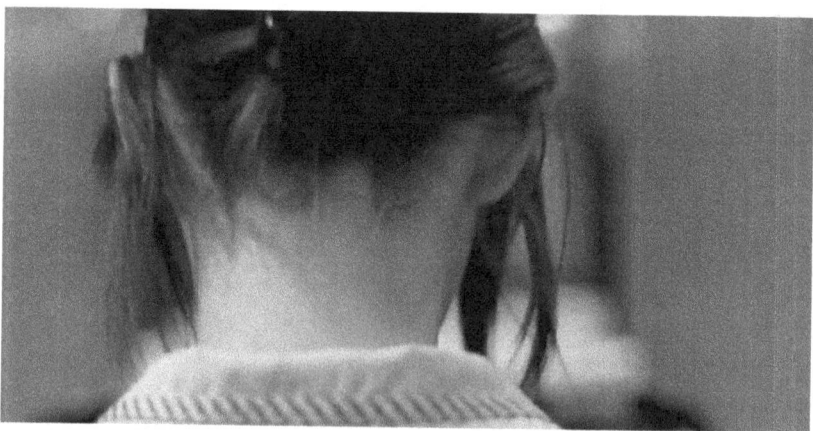

Fig. 6

Another close-up of Christelle's legs as she walks down stairs show her practical black shoes, following her further into the depths of the hotel. In the employee locker room, she rubs hotel cream onto her hands – a stash is lined up in her locker, another reminder of the separation between her and the guests. Standing half-undressed at a line of sinks, she lifts her feet one at a time under the running tap and massages them. She alternates looking down at her feet and at her face in the mirror, worn out from her day. Positioned behind a tall trolley stacked with linen behind her, which partially obscures the shot, we observe a private moment, one that is presumably part of her daily routine (Fig. 7). This intimate moment of bathing is reminiscent of work by Edgar Degas, whose models often held awkward poses, like Christelle, in an effort to convey a sense of realism. Later scenes of June in the hotel bath and Coré being bathed tie the three women together, showing how different their experiences of the world are.

Fig. 7

In a corridor painted in garish blue and white, filled with stacks of cane chairs, a blurred smudge of someone in the far background comes in and turns a corner in about a second. A creak signals a door opening off-screen, prompting an extreme close-up of Christelle's face, her eyes moving in response to the same sound, heard over the dripping tap. We still hear this dripping as the camera moves to an upstairs corridor, another contrast between the spaces. Shane lays face-down on the bed in the dark masturbating while the shower runs. Is he thinking about his wife, just a few meters away, or Christelle? In the warmly-lit bathroom, fluffy his-and-hers bathrobes are reflected in the mirror, along with the couple's toiletries, including those from the hotel Christelle was just using. A shot of June's legs standing in the shallow bath again emphasises the parallel with Christelle. Shane reaches for a tiny bottle and shakes out a pill, indicating again that whatever is wrong with him is tied to sexual activity. Leaving the dark of the windowless room, Christelle offers her first smile as she rushes out to a man on motorcycle, who she kisses. The tension of the bathroom scene, with its unseen intruder, was not about a present danger but is instead prophetic. A final close-up of the pill bottle reminds of Shane's search for a medical cure.

THE LAB

On the window sill of a brightly-lit and sterile lab sit two pot plants, a plant in a plastic bottle and a small glass container filled with liquid in which a rod spins, its rotations emitting a distinct clicking. The deeper hum of running equipment continues throughout the scene. A bucket holds a brain submerged in liquid, its surface rippling. Another brain is carefully sliced into segments by a long knife held by gloved hands – a utilitarian garment so different to June's pretty gloves (Fig. 8). Choart (José Garcia) – wearing mask and goggles – concentrates on his meticulous, delicate work. A circular view through a microscope lens is accompanied by a distant voice. Malécot, who is studying this slide, is hearing Shane speaking through the phone left off the hook (these are the first words in over six minutes). Choart tells Malécot he does not have time for the call, followed by a final close-up of tweezers extracting veins from the brain tissue. These steady, lingering shots of brains are unnerving reminders that individuals are, in fact, meat. They also suggest the biological nature of whatever disease Coré and Shane seem to share, which must be tied to this very lab. Sitting on the floor leaning against the bed, Shane thanks Malécot. There is one drip from a tap.

THE BATH – JUNE

The camera moves slowly along June's body in the bath, taking thirty seconds to reach from her feet to face. Her wedding band is prominent on her hand. The sense of

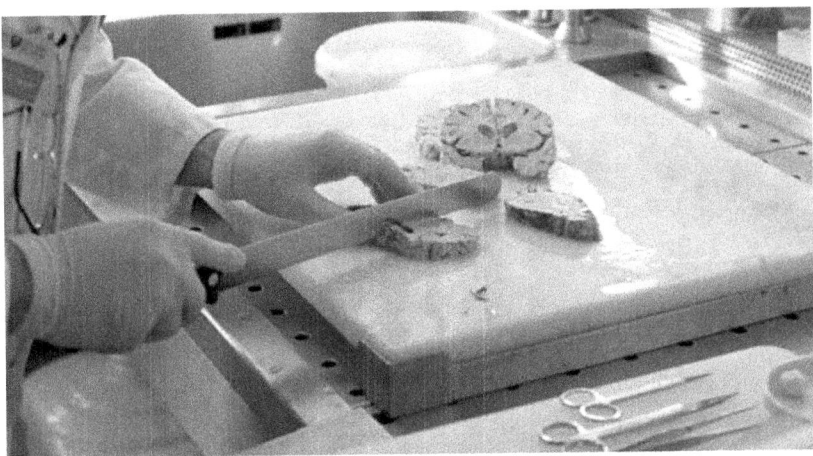

Fig. 8

relaxation here, soaking in the water for pleasure not necessity, uncomfortably recalls Christelle washing her feet at the sink downstairs after having cleaned this bath. Tindersticks' 'Seaweed' inspired the shot of June's public hair moving in the water, with Denis explaining that 'through this song, I could dream a body like a landscape...and therefore a body that could be destroyed' (in Le Vern 2018). This reflects a central idea in the film, that the body is fragile and, when viewed as an object, unbound from personality, is easily broken. The next shot hints at this danger, the camera cutting abruptly to Shane's face staring down at June followed by a close-up of her pubic hair. Prescient of Christelle's final scene, Shane edges closer to giving into his hunger. June's face is submerged below the water, her eyes closed, distorted by the lapping water (Fig. 9). Lifting her head, she is startled by his presence. A wider shot turns up towards Shane's intimidating gaze, emphasising his discomfort as he noticeably swallows. Staring down at her, in a clear position of power, his expression is unreadable but chilling (Fig. 10). June exudes vulnerability, hinting that she might end up bathing in blood like in Shane's terrible fantasies. Yet, the camera lowers as he kneels beside the bath, and audibly exhales, suppressing this feeling for the moment. 'Are you frightened?' he asks, stroking her head, soothing her about a danger she is only just starting to grasp. She responds with her own question: 'who were you calling?' to which he replies 'Some boss in a lab'. June leans up to kiss him. Out of the bath, he wraps her in a robe and hugs her

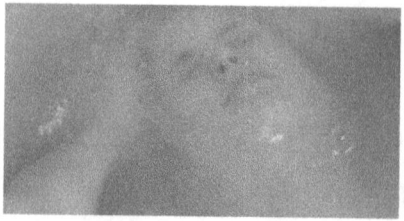 

Figs. 9 & 10

tightly, conveying a care and protection reminiscent of drawing the blanket over her on the plane. Yet, holding her arm draws attention to a bite mark, framed by his thumb and forefingers. She looks at it, skin bruised and red, his body imprinted on hers, both memory and warning. 'Let's go,' he says.

ESCAPE

Coré moves into a shot of an empty field, again dressed in slip, boots and coat. A small skip, gleeful and childlike, captures the joy of escape. Lifting her coat up, like a cape, she tips her head back and emits a guttural growl. A vampiric figure, she evokes iconic images like Bela Lugosi as *Dracula* (Browning, 1931) and Marfa performing in a bat costume in *Les Vampires* (Feuillade, 1915). As Léo rides his motorcycle home, a version of the theme song plays, a brief aural warning of Coré's activities. Unlike Léo, whose daily life is consumed by constant threat, Erwan has little to worry about as he lies on his bed beside his friend, sharing a cigarette. They listen to the motorcycle as Léo returns home – 'like clockwork' says Erwan, who is obviously still planning to break in, fascinated by what is inside the mysterious house. Right now, it is nothing: the house has not been able to contain the horror inside, the monster has escaped. The front door is open, the electric saw still audibly running. Following Léo's feet upstairs, he finds a ragged hole carved in the bedroom door and the room trashed, the mattress sliced open and furnishings and fabric strewn around. In the empty garage, Léo smokes a cigarette by himself, which is not a way to just pass the time like for Erwan, but to prepare for what comes next.

Again in a field at night, a close-up of a blade of tall grass dripping with blood is followed by wider shots revealing large patches of blood-soaked ground. Denis says they spent three hours filming these drops of blood on the grass (in Gonzalez 2001). Behind a screen of grass, Léo digs, the sound of his hoe and shovel hitting the earth mixed with his grunts of effort. Sitting in the van, blood on her face and tears in her eyes, Coré mouths something inaudibly. The repetition of Léo's actions here suggests that they have performed this routine many times before: she escapes and kills; he chases and covers for her. His exertion also implies the emotional strain of this work. In the hotel corridor, quiet and dim at night, Shane and June's door is a portent of the future. A parallel to the open door of the house Coré escaped, this room still contains Shane and his desires. Inside, a romantic scene of the couple asleep, arms entwined, is disturbed as Shane switches on the lamp to light a cigarette, which he smokes in the dark, a distraction from his increasingly strong urges.

THE BATH – CORÉ

Fig. 11

Léo dips a sponge into water tinged red with fresh blood, his hands a reminder of his complicity in Coré's murders. She lies naked and still as he bathes her, submitting to his gentle but firm movements, clearly familiar with the process (Fig. 11). This is an act of love as well as responsibility. It might be their bond that ensures she does not attack, or she might simply be sated. Unlike June in the hotel bath, soaking for pleasure, Coré's blood-streaked body being bathed signals the presence of abjection. The polluted body is not just about being unclean or unhealthy, but a complete disruption of order, of rules and identity. The bath here is more than a sign of being unwashed, but of something very wrong. Of particular importance is that it is here Coré speaks her only line in the film. Holding her husband's hand, she looks at him and whispers 'I don't want to wait anymore, Léo. I want to die.' Her affliction has not completely taken over her mind; something of her former self survives. In this moment of lucidity, Coré is aware of what she has become and can no longer bear it.

Lying in bed, Erwan watches the light creeping through the shutters of the Semeneaus bedroom, tempted by the mystery hidden in that room, which stories like Pandora's Box and Bluebeard have taught us never ends well. He is so taken with Coré because she is so obviously forbidden and he needs to know why. Shane, meanwhile, is also not sleeping but stands on the hotel balcony in the dark, lit an eerie shade of yellow-green, the sound of traffic humming below. Again, he rubs his face, obviously tired. While it could be jetlag, perhaps he is too agitated to sleep because of his blood-soaked dreams. Léo also forgoes sleep, retreating to his indoor greenhouse. Seen at work through the plastic sheeting, another window of sorts, he researches a cure for Coré. A brief abstract shot of speeding down the road at night, the white centre markings recognisable only when accompanied by the sound of a vehicle wooshing down a highway, reveals a split-second glimpse of Shane staring out the window of his hotel.

HOTEL

Shane looks out the window, then back at the sleeping June, in almost completely darkness. Before dawn, Christelle arrives at the hotel on the back of a motorcycle, kisses the driver and walks into the employee entrance with her colleagues. June stirs at the click of the door as Shane leaves. In the locker room, the maids change into their uniforms. Like Danny leading us through the hallway on his tricycle in *The Shining*, we again follow the back of Christelle's neck as she pushes her trolley along the corridors, its wheels whirring. Outside the Brownses room, the "do not disturb" sign on the door brings to mind Danny's first encounter with room 237. Inside, June is mumbling in French in her sleep when she is awoken by a beep. Opening Shane's computer, bite mark still prominent on her arm, she finds a list of email bounce-backs for various addresses for Léo.

LAB

Having been ignored over the phone, Shane has gone to the lab in person. Though Choart protests to Malécot that this is harassment, the men sit down for what is the longest and most informative conversation in the film so far. The rhythmic tapping of an agitator again emphasises the work that is happening in the sanitised white room. Choart explains that he took the job running the lab after Léo left the city with no warning, cutting all ties. When Shane mentions a controversial paper he wrote, the spinning sound quickens, anticipating a revelation. Choart is sceptical of Shane and derisive of Léo: 'The truth of the matter is, Semeneau is no longer part of the scientific community. Try the talk show circuit, maybe.' Shane again rubs his face, accepting a glass of water. Choart switches off the agitator, the abrupt quiet signalling the end of the conversation. Shane leaves, passing the garden with plant labels, presumably where the lab grows its biological materials. Close-ups of apparatus throughout this scene remind us that Shane is from the scientific community. But, plagued by dreams of blood and death, he is already progressing beyond the world of methodology and reason, which offers no assistance, to one of emotion and instinct.

HOTEL

Wearing gloves and a black cape, with the hood drawn, June greets the maids in the corridor, including Christelle, whose arm she touches in an overly-familiar way. Like when she helped make the bed, June ignores the division that should exist between staff and guests. Elsewhere, Shane crosses a boundary, spying on a woman applying lipstick at a mirror. Drawing attention to her lips, this everyday act signals her attractiveness and hints at sex. As she tries to leave, Shane moves into the narrow doorway, creating the opportunity to push against and grope her. Shoving him away, she admonishes 'You psycho'. Shane seems to be losing his ability to control himself. With the Brownses room unoccupied, Christelle again makes the bed and scrubs the bath. Pausing for a moment, she looks incredibly sad. The camera tracks slowly down the corridor lined with trolleys, with something predatory about the pace – it is Shane, returning to the room. Taking off his coat, he gets into bed fully dressed. Christelle apologises and quickly leaves. Again, the divide between staff and guests, inside and outside, is disturbed by their presence in the same space, even briefly. While her labour is essential, it should be invisible. However, an unusual precedent was established by the Brownses early arrival, creating an uncomfortable familiarity between the three characters. This confusion of boundaries puts Christelle in an awkward and – eventually – fatal position.

FLASHBACKS

A flashback scene offers the primary source of exposition in the film. Documentary-style footage is shot with a different film stock, shaky and grainy with a light leak at the end, bleeding yellow like an old film reel. In a lab, close-ups show test tubes, bottles and beakers filled with plant specimens. One label reads FRIESSEN – a Luxembourgish word which means to eat, or to gorge, an obscure but appropriate reference. The loud steady whirr of the machines is punctuated by sounds like liquids sloshing and bubbling, which continue throughout Shane's uncomfortable conversation with a woman in a lab coat. It reveals that after graduate school, Shane worked for Universal Pharmacon, chosen solely as they made the best offer. Reading of Léo's work, he convinced his boss to let him take supplies and money to Guyana where Léo had assembled a team of experts, including Coré Cordrine (which the woman pointedly corrects to 'Mrs Léo Semeneau'). Shane denies he had an affair with Coré, though admits he wished he had. The woman grills him:

> 'Do you believe in loyalty, Mr Brown? What about betrayal? What's you stance about betrayal, Mr Brown?'

> 'You were not there. You don't know what happened. You don't know me. You're wrong.'

'Wasn't I? Semeneau was against experimenting with human beings and you knew it, but, huge profits were to be made, Mr Brown, and you like money and you're a man in a hurry so you stole Léo's work. Now get out of here.'

The camera returns to Shane in bed, emphasizing this was a memory, perhaps from earlier in the day. He opens his laptop, revealing a page detailing Léo as a researcher of botany and neuroscience who, after leading a bioprospecting mission in 1990, published an article predicting 'these samples and analyses should in the near future help us to focus our pharmacological research into nervous diseases, pain, mental diseases and problems of libido'. Shane clicks to enlarge Léo's photo, cutting to another flashback, an older memory, from Guyana.

Fig. 12

A shaky handheld camera pans across a misty treeline before pushing through ferns on the rainforest floor. Filmed on a different stock again, potentially digicam, it evokes archival footage, grainy and drained of colour (Fig. 12). It is the research expedition in the jungle, a glimpse of a shared past. Located on the north-east coast of South America, Guyana has one of the largest unspoiled rainforests in the world. Some areas are almost inaccessible by humans, which appealed to European explorers of the region such as Sir Walter Raleigh. Western history is filled with stories of men venturing into remote and dangerous terrain, part of a long tradition of exploration and colonisation. Popular interest in such stories is reflected in adventure films, especially in the 1930s and

1940s, where characters search for lost treasures or family members and survive plane crashes or shipwrecks, jungle animals and bloodthirsty tribes.

The subject is central to the Italian cannibal exploitation subgenre, which peaked in the decade between 1972 and 1982, a series of low-budget films often banned due to their extreme violence and gore (discussed in chapter 4). Mostly set in the Amazon, these are largely predicated on the danger of venturing into the unknown, reflecting a fear of the Other. Of course, this sequence also draws from the history of scientific research in these regions, with expeditions focused on sourcing natural products to be studied and synthesised. Yet, the camp in Guyana seems very far from corporate offices or even the lab where Choart and Malécot work. A makeshift lab is set up outdoors, with rows of specimens planted in tin cans contrasting to earlier shots of polished beakers and test tubes. A final close-up glides up one stem to reveal a pair of shiny green leaves – this must be the origin of Coré and Shane's affliction. A ringing phone disturbs this vestige of the past, though the call brings Shane closer to it as it is Malécot arranging to meet him. Arriving mid-conversation, June waits so she can listen in unnoticed.

NOTRE-DAME

A steep shot up towards Notre-Dame Cathedral moves down to reveal Shane hugging June, who appear like typical newlyweds sightseeing in Paris. An exception to the mostly mundane settings in the film, this recognisable landmark foregrounds the beauty of Paris, a destination for lovers. The loud tolling of the bells situates both characters and viewers, overlaying a series of architectural close-ups reminding of the cathedrals history, a place of devotion and penitence, right and wrong, redemption and damnation. In the Last Judgment portal, Archangel Michael holds the scales that weigh souls, guiding the virtuous to heaven – the devil to his left takes the condemned to hell. An extreme close-up of a hand grasping an ankle and another of two gargoyles, mouths agape displaying sharp fangs, engender a sense of discomfort, warning of danger. These images are offset by Shane's comical behaviour as he enacts a sequence of references to classic horror cinema, the only time he displays any type of personality, other than anxious brooding. On the balcony, he picks June up like Quasimodo from *The Hunchback of Notre Dame* (Worsley, 1923), and she plays along, laughing. He lurches towards her, arms outstretched like Frankenstein's monster, and she raises her arms in a pantomime of a classic horror victim (Fig. 13). She has no idea how close she is to taking on that role for real. From her point of view, he snarls and contorts his hands like a vampire, recalling Bela Lugosi's Dracula and also Lon Chaney as a hypnotist in *London after Midnight* (Browning, 1927). While Gallo's exaggerated and humorous impressions seem incongruously out of place in tone, they offer a brief moment of respite before the true horror that is to follow.

Fig. 13

The camera switches between June and Shane's points of view, engendering a sense of intimacy, allowing the audience to share their experience. Leaning against a gargoyle, June unwinds a sheer green scarf from around her head and Shane takes her photograph. Without the lens between them, he looks at her seriously, and she returns the look – like Léo and Coré, they share a private wordless message. The scarf shudders precariously in the breeze and Shane leans over the edge only to see it slip away. Its flight across the city offers a stunning aerial view of Paris, a sequence marked by melancholy. Beautiful and ephemeral, the scarf evokes the fragility of life and, more specifically, the body. This decisive moment confirms Shane is losing his grasp on his life and perhaps on June, whose pale, smooth skin is as delicate as the scarf. Stress is palpable on Shane's face. Back at the hotel, in bed, they hold hands, lit by an eerie blue-green light (Fig. 14). Looking over June's shoulder reveals Shane with one eye open, watching her. He whispers another promise: 'I'll never hurt you. I like you, June'. Sleepily she replies 'hmm? I like you too', clearly unaware of the true implications of this declaration.

Fig. 14

CORÉ AND ERWAN

Erwan looks up at the window shutters; Coré looks out from her dark room. He pulls off the bar of a downstairs window, smashes the glass and he and his friend break in. Upstairs, Coré lies on her back, listening, waiting. They enter the lab, opening the industrial fridges stocked with specimens and a freezer where they discover a brain in dry ice – even this does not compel them to turn around. Erwan is pointedly insolent, dropping a test tube and eating something from a jar (which he then spits out on the floor), two potentially hazardous actions showing his recklessness. He then eats an apple, an impudent, if minor, act of stealing that proves he will help himself to whatever he wants in the house. The apple, of course, is a recognisable symbol of dangerous temptation, recalling the Garden of Eden, Snow White and the Apple of Discord. Upstairs from the clean and ordered lab, filled with expensive equipment, the interior is in a state of disrepair, with crumbling walls and peeling paint. When Erwan heads up the main staircase, his friend, shrewdly, refuses to follow, taking heed of an instinct that warns of the danger of venturing further into the house. This is another moment familiar from horror films, when a rational and prescient warning is ignored. Erwan enacts the role of the fairy-tale hero, ascending through the castle to save the woman imprisoned inside, with the expectation of her wholehearted gratitude (usually expressed as a kiss). Well-versed in seduction, Coré promises much more without speaking a word.

Coré slowly creeps into view, visible through the apertures in the hastily boarded up door (Fig. 15). Erwan walks up to her, followed by a reverse shot toward him. Sliding her fingers out a gap, she laces them through his, rubbing his hands; he closes his eyes, his breathing getting heavier. From beside him, we watch her put his finger in her mouth. He steps back abruptly and her hand creeps out the hole. Then they are trying to kiss and it is now her breathing that is audibly heavy. As Erwan frantically pulls away the boards, like he did with the bars downstairs, Coré stands disquietingly silent and still. A close-up shows her seductively pull the sheer white fabric of her nightdress up her thighs to reveal her naked beneath it, hidden by shadows. Through the gap, his eyes appear desperate as he yanks away the board in front of his face, breathing heavily from exertion and desire. He steps through the doorway, unaware that in crossing that border he has signed his own death sentence.

Fig. 15

Coré's breathing is the overwhelming sound as the camera travels slowly across skin, highlighting hair and moles on parts of body that are not always identifiable. She runs her hand across Erwan, whose eyes are closed. When she leans down, her shadow covers him and the screen is reduced to black. Her open mouth runs along him and then they kiss. She straddles him, the edge of her dress barely covering them as they have sex. Downstairs, the friend waits. Soft percussion on the soundtrack is joined by the deep reverberation of a cello. Filmed almost entirely in the dark, the camera so close to the bodies that it is difficult to see what is happening, the scene becomes overwhelmingly claustrophobic. Coré becomes increasingly aggressive, licking Erwan's chin then biting it, at which point he begins to resist. She holds his face, hands around his neck. Leaning in, the screen becomes almost completely black, focusing attention on the sound of him choking, which turns to a strangled cry as she chews his neck. A close-up of his face streaked with blood moves to an extreme close-up of his mouth as he screams. In a brief moment of reprieve, we return to Erwan's friend, who begins to worry that the screams might not be of pleasure. Peering up through the bannister, the staircase still a barrier he is unwilling to cross. When Coré yelps like an animal, he leaves. In the bedroom, Coré is chewing on Erwan's face, which is mangled like the truck driver's. By this point, the sound is clearer and more upsetting than the images, with Erwan alternating between sobbing and screaming, clearly in pain, a horrific contrast to the soft Tindersticks soundtrack in the background. Coré is not finished - she slaps at his face, screams back at him, also crying. In a second brief diversion, Shane drinks something from a vial before finishing his coffee standing at the bar of a café. In the bedroom, the music has stopped, drawing attention to Erwan's dying gasps and Coré's giggling and sighing. She laps blood from his chest, licks his face, kisses him. In a final, horrible transgression, she sticks her finger in a flap of skin, an act of penetration that leads her to orgasm.

This excruciatingly long and visceral scene is rendered in close proximity to the viewer. Yves Domenjoud supervised the special effects, which included a blood pump on Erwan's neck and the fake flesh on his cheek. There were no rehearsals and they only did one take. Denis explains that she, the actors and the crew shared a sense of the unknown when filming the scene: 'I had the word "devour" in my head... As long as we followed the stroke of Beatrice's hand on his body we could accompany that scene as a crew... It was not funny at all. Not funny like in a horror film where a vampire comes to a girl and sucks her neck. There was something about the "devouring" of the young man; yesterday we spoke about the English word "surrender". He surrendered, he did not defend himself anymore' (in Vecchio 2014). Dalle admits that 'seeing the fear in his eyes was unnerving. The state we were in by the end of the scene was astonishing – we were in bits. But I'm very proud of the fact that we both surrendered to the moment and didn't stop and break the intensity' (in Dawson 2002). Denis also emphasises that she concentrated on the wellbeing of the actors, in both this scene and the later locker room scene, concerned about their suffering or feeling too exposed, an attitude that contrasts to some directors of challenging films, who push their actors uncomfortably to achieve great performances.

THE ADDRESS

As Shane drinks another coffee, Malécot taps on the window, beckoning him. She passes on an address for the Semenaus, explaining Léo needs a friend as his wife is very sick, so he works at home to take care of her. Shane again puts his head in his hands, and, once he walks away, we see that Malécot immediately regrets her actions. In a flashback, Coré, just visible on the edge of the frame, places her hand on Malécot's shoulder and asks for a cigarette, which she passes across and lights. As Coré exhales and thanks her, Malécot's smile radiates warmth. Placing the women in such close proximity, the camera just behind Coré's shoulder, highlights how people respond to her presence, how she seduced them even then. Overlaying Malécot's smile we hear Léo saying in French 'I need six months', cutting to a scene where he asks Choart for a favour. 'Do it for Coré at least. Do it for her,' he pleads. An extreme close-up conveys his distress, matched by another of Choart who replies 'I can't', shaking his head. Then, there is a close-up of Coré – the only time in the film we see her face before her transformation. She wears make-up and her hair is styled in a neat bob – this must be how Malécot recalls her.

Malécot finds a payphone and the dial tone switches to the ring of a telephone inside the house. Coré paces in front of a wall she has painted in blood, ghastly art which is a continuation of her fervent immersion in the flesh. Her white dress splattered with blood is a familiar image from gothic literature and films as varied as *Carrie* (De Palma, 1976), *Valerie and Her Week of Wonders* (Jires, 1970) and any number of examples from

Hammer horror. Coré's movements recall a dance of sorts, her fingers outstretched and hands gesturing in a way that resembles some arcane ritual. The abstract symbols she has painted recall sigils, invoking a supernatural realm, a fantastical world of blood magic. A similar trope is the killer who scrawls messages in victims' blood. Coré, as we have seen, has moved almost entirely beyond language, instead expressing herself in a non-verbal way. Her emphasis on gesture, driven by instinct, suggests she has devised her own form of Abstract Expressionism, a movement that sought access to a primal and universal experience (discussed in more detail in chapter 4).

SHANE AND CORÉ

A dog looks out of a car window, behind which sits Shane, watching buildings pass by as he ventures out to the suburbs. Arriving at the house, he looks through the fence before jumping over the side wall, like Erwan. Seen from outside in more detail, the tall gate echoes those guarding mansions in gothic novels. The broken window signals what has come before, that Erwan entered but never left. Inside, Coré appears on the staircase, a site where women are positioned to be looked at in cinema, presented for the gaze of onlookers, both inside and outside the world of the film. She hesitantly points her toe before slowly descending, clasping at her dress and wrist, tentative and confused. It is as if she is intoxicated, impaired by her indulgence in blood and flesh. If her condition is neurological, which is certainly seems to be, it follows that the endorphins triggered by sex might be different for her. Maybe her heightened sex drive is matched by a steep comedown. The shuffling of her bare feet is audible in the quiet house. Backing into the shadows, Shane watches her. Like when he accosted the woman in the earlier scene, he covertly surveys his prey. Coré tentatively roams through her house, revealing the extent of its disrepair. A close-up of Shane's face emerges from the darkness, a sinister Baroque portrait, terrified by what he sees, a premonition of what he will become. Coré turns directly towards the camera before walking past it, revealing her blood-smeared face up-close. She finds what she was looking for: matches. Striking one, she emerges from the black like Shane; holding the light to her face, she stares into the flames that she intends to consume her (Fig. 16). Léo rides through a tunnel, his helmet visor lifted to reveal his face.

Fig. 16

Shane approaches Coré, who joyfully embraces him. She clutches at him, putting her hands on either side of face and lifting his arm around her so he is holding her back. He responds by repeating the phrase 'I'm sick', almost in a sob. Her instincts take over and she pulls at the back of his shirt, reaching for his throat. 'Hey, come on,' he says, pushing her away. She screams in frustration at the thwarted attack, baring her teeth and making guttural noises as his hands squeeze her throat. The intensifying hue of the eerie yellow background is a fire, which is now audibly crackling as it spreads. Shane pushes Coré to the floor and strangles her, before moving away to leave us above her lifeless body as it is engulfed by flames. The fire reaches the bed and pillow stained with blood, destroying the evidence of her earlier activities. Léo enters the burning house, with the final shot of him squinting through the flames – it is too late. The fire seems biblical, purifying, with Coré burning like a witch or supernatural creature. The transgressive woman is punished, but the man, it seems, has escaped his punishment.

SHANE AT NIGHT

Shane is overwhelmed by violent feelings, bound up with desire, fuelled by the murder which is, we assume, his first. A close-up of him nuzzling June progresses to another sex scene which echoes that between Coré and Erwan, close-ups of hands on skin, unidentifiable parts of the body – knees, hands, a mix of limbs – all treated with a haptic lens that draws attention to the texture of the skin, warm and alive. Yet, their clasped ringed hands emphasise this union is within marriage. An intimate close-up of June's eyes and then he is gone, fleeing from the impulse to hurt her like he did Coré. In the bathroom, we see and hear Shane masturbating – a close-up of his face showing he is pained, almost crying, as he keeps looking up towards the door, against which June leads her forehead from the other side, listening. Ejaculate arcs across the sink (a scene which, unsurprisingly, critics did not care for). June bangs her palm against the closed door, sobbing and yelling his name. He pulls on a jumper and, when he opens the door, pushes her out of the way. June lies on the floor, beside herself, a scene reminiscent of a mid-twentieth-century melodrama (Fig. 17).

Fig. 17

Shane heads unsteadily down stairs into the night, echoing his emotional descent. The sound of heels signals a woman just before she walks past us. A close-up of her face is matched by one of Shane who is behind her, his stride silent. This familiar scene of a woman being followed down the street is especially tense as it is clear now what Shane is capable of. In the hotel, June looks at the ejaculate marking the mirror, reaching down to touch it, rubbing it between her fingers, viscous evidence of what is wrong between them. Her uncertainty and desperation for answers lead her outside, where, still wearing only her bathrobe, she stands in the rain. Bringing her an umbrella, the doorman guides her back inside. Here, she makes a choice: search for answers. Opening Shane's bag, she discovers a startling collection of various bottles of pills, unlabelled and presumably trials from his work. Using his Palm Pilot, she finds a contact for 'Jeanne', which she calls and is answered by a French-speaking woman.

The gently lapping water of the Seine is stained pink, signalling the dawn, much like the opening scene. Shane lies on a bench by the water, where he has spent the rest of the night. Passing a pet store, he is drawn to the puppies in the window. On a bus, he cradles and pats one he purchased (a discomforting scene for anyone who has seen *American Psycho* [Harron, 2000]). Shane's loss of boundaries and his increasingly predatory nature is conveyed in a sequence of images. A close-up of the back of a woman's head, the nape of her neck covered by her collar, echoes the images of Christelle's neck. Standing behind her in the aisle, Shane moves closer until his nose almost touches her neck. A young woman (Alice Houri) seated nearby pointedly watches him – he glares at her until she looks away. The way he makes this banal activity of catching a bus dangerous surely resonates with many women who frequently experience similarly inappropriate behaviour in public, feeling uncomfortable and, sometimes, unsafe. At the hotel, Christelle kisses another woman hello in the locker room, a portent of the upcoming scene.

JEANNE

'June Brown? It sounds nice together,' says Jeanne as she makes tea in her robe, graciously hospitable considering it is obviously very early. June stands by a window in a study wearing a cream suit and red gloves, an outfit that sums her up – buttoned-up purity punctuated by a sense of determination. It seems old fashioned and overly demure, such a contrast to Coré. Jeanne is an old friend of Shane's who used to rent him a room in the house but has not seen him in a long time; it is not the affair June was worried about. Enveloped by the warmth of a home after the personality-less hotel room, a sleepless night and potentially relief at Jeanne's warm welcome, June falls asleep mid-conversation. A close-up draws attention to a new cut on her lip, a mark to match that on her arm, kisses getting closer to bites. Jeanne hands over a box of Shane's old belongings, mementos of a time before June. Pointing to a photo of Léo and another of Shane, she asks 'Has he changed much?' June replies 'I wouldn't know', prompting the uncomfortable question she must be asking herself: can you ever really know someone?

CHRISTELLE AND SHANE

The maids again perform the never-ending task of cleaning the hotel, of removing the traces left behind by its many visitors. In the Brownses room, Christelle lies down on the freshly-made bed. She touches the scarf hung over the bedside lamp, presumably by June, a predictable tourist souvenir printed with images of the *Mona Lisa*. Loosening her hair from its clip, she even steals a cigarette which she smokes, the image of insouciance (Fig. 18). Like Erwan eating the apple, this is a slightly rebellious way to pass the time, a sign of boredom as much as desire. It is a challenge to the couple to notice and a gamble they will not say anything. Picking up a note left on the table, she reads it before throwing it on the bed. While hotel rooms are supposed to feel private and safe for the comfort of guests, this scene reminds that they are not. Staff have access to room keys and enter daily, touching items like linen and towels, with which guests have been physically close, and performing activities that are in close contact with intimate aspects of daily life, such as making the bed and cleaning the bathroom. Yet, it is Shane who is the danger here, again lurking in the shadows as he watches Christelle leave his room, putting her hair back up to continue with her day. That he is now nuzzling a puppy only heightens his sinister stare. He finds the note on the bed, which is from June asking where he is. There is an obvious indent in the bedspread which he lies on top of, face down, smelling, as if preparing to track his prey (Fig. 19).

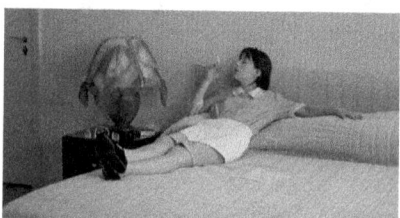 

Fig. 18 & 19

The following locker room scene is close to, if not actually, unwatchable, sitting alongside Gaspar Noe's *Irreversible* (2002) in terms of a visceral, painful crossing of boundaries, an on-screen trauma that leaves an indelible mark on the viewer. It is not a scene to be watched without careful consideration about the subject – Christelle's rape and murder – which the following two paragraphs detail. We track across Christelle's profile as she pushes her trolley downstairs, again with the wheels clicking. Another predatory shot of the back of her neck shows her entering the dark locker room. The sense of repetition makes Shane's intrusion more surprising. Christelle again takes out her hair, another close-up of the back of her neck moving down to her shoulder as she takes off her shirt. A shot from above the lockers reveals the top half of Shane's face in profile as he passes by, stalking her. From behind him, we see her notice him. She holds her locker, but when he reaches out to stroke her face, she rubs her cheek across it briefly, then lets him pull her towards him. She looks down at his arm as he wraps it around her bare waist and visibly goes limp. There is no sign of consent here and he is certainly in the position of power – she is smaller, half-dressed and an employee of the hotel.

Shane embraces Christelle, who puts her arms around his neck and as he holds her wrists she fights back gently, smiling slightly. But as he becomes more aggressive, pushing her against the locker, she struggles. He holds her head and kisses her, pushing her to ground where, as when murdering Coré, his body obscures much of the shot. He pulls off her underwear, leaving her exposed, and rapes her, as she yells and fights back. Still holding her down, he moves down to perform cunnilingus where, thankfully, his actions are partially obscured as she starts to scream properly. The camera alternates between this angle and her face as she cries, with her effort obvious in her hands pushing at him and her screams, a horrifying closeness echoing the scene between Coré and Erwan. A shot of Christelle's face upside down, screaming, is a trope in horror films, including from the iconic opening of *Suspiria* (1977). Her point of view, a shot of his head, is much more typical to pornography – when Shane lifts his head, his mouth is covered in blood, a vampiric image. Exactly like Coré, he leans down to kiss her, panting, then orgasms as he kisses her face, wiping blood over it. Again, this scene is, thankfully, mostly dark at this point. Her bloody face is the only thing visible – the view of the rest of her body cut off by the locker and then dragged offscreen, leaving a trail of blood on the floor. Shane wipes his face and hands on the linens on the cart, recalling when he held the edge of the sheet Christelle was using to make the bed, his intentions clear from their very first meeting.

CLEAN

The sound of whimpering, an aural reminder of Christelle's pain, reveals the puppy as June returns to the hotel room. Putting down her red purse, that matches her shoes and gloves, she crouches down to pick it up and comfort it. Hearing the shower running, she calls Shane's name. He wipes streaks of blood off the shower curtain. In the mirror, we see her enter, hesitantly. The water is turned off, followed by an ominous shot of June looking up towards him, small in contrast to the indistinct figure looming in the foreground behind the opaque curtain (Fig. 20). Cutting to a close-up of his face, June asks 'How are you feeling doc?' 'I feel good,' he replies with a half-smile, and pulls her into a hug. A drop of blood slides down the curtain as he says: 'I want to go home.' 'OK,' she replies, as the drip continues to trail down the curtain. Shane's gaze follows hers towards it and he puts his head on hers. The final shot is a close-up of June's eyes, which she scrunches closed before opening them again. If the story so far was Shane's, it is now hers and the film closes with the unanswered question of what she will do next.

Fig. 20

3. BORDERS/BODIES: SPACE, SURFACE, TOUCH AND DESIRE

Trouble Every Day is governed by, even obsessed with, the idea of the border, which is tied to its representation of bodies. It interrogates the relationship between inside and outside, exploring the intersection of image, gaze, screen, surface, touch, skin and desire. This is visually established by the spatial organisation of the film, where the locations we frequent – hotel suite, lab, bedroom, locker room – are almost entirely private places that we enter unbidden. On a corporeal level, skin is a phenomenological border that the camera roams, sometimes so close-up that body parts are unidentifiable. The lens lingers on the skin as well as what it produces when it is penetrated, the epidermis pierced to reveal wounds and blood, abject signs of bodily violation. The treatment of the body produces a physical response in the viewer, the camera engendering a reciprocity between celluloid and physical bodies. Denis and Godard ensure that this relationship between character and viewer is not just narrative but haptic. The emphasis on surfaces, on engaging the senses – especially touch – is informed by the Baroque and also the Rococo, art movements that immerse viewers in fictive worlds. Similarly, *Trouble Every Day* features an identifiable and concrete narrative world into which Denis pulls the audience, one that is also shaped by violence and desire. Treating the strange happenings as indisputably real lays the groundwork for fantasy taken to extremes; unspeakable desire manifests in the world in a way that it should not be able to, perilously uncontrolled. Expressed as hunger, it leads from kissing to biting to eating, with the eventual cannibalism reflecting the pursuit of complete incorporation.

SCRIPT, PRODUCTION DESIGN AND SOUND

Trouble Every Day is both immersive, not allowing the viewer to escape the world of the film, but also closed off, almost painfully obscure. This paradox arises in part as the viewer is assumed to be part of the diegetic world, so very little background is offered in the first act, with the narrative shuttered in on itself. Denis does not lay out the story but hints at it, leaving us to search for more. She makes viewers work to come up with their own narratives, using not just what they are told but what they are not. The film is about what is unsaid as much as what is said; meaning is found through the gaps Denis leaves. She acknowledges that when writing, 'often we do a first draft that has no gaps and then I feel it doesn't sound musical or interesting to me. So then I cut' (in Smith 2005). Even the explanatory scenes are not explicit. In particular, there is no clear sense of a timeline. Was the trip to Guyana a year ago, or several years ago? How long since the three scientists have seen each other? How long has Coré been murdering people? How long has Shane been affected? Has Shane also been murdering people in America? How long has June known Shane? While the film leaves us to fill in these blanks ourselves, it offers very few objects in the mise-en-scène, such as television screens, book covers or art, which might provide clues.

The production design in Trouble Every Day is understated, prioritising realism. Concrete and familiar settings ground the strange behaviour, which is treated as absolutely real. Denis and Godard decided on the locations together and began shooting in January 2000. The interior of the hotel is the InterContinental Paris Le Grand Hotel. Coré and Léo's house is a nineteenth-century building in Raincy, a residential area in the eastern suburbs of Paris, which had recently been a shelter for young offenders leaving prison – half of the ground floor had been burned. Dalle describes the building as charged with history: 'There was no need to say "quiet" on set – you felt silenced by the atmosphere' (in Dawson 2002). A preoccupation with architectural space pervades Trouble Every Day, with the interiors revealed slowly, fragmented in a way to create a sense of unease. The long scenes moving through the corridors of the hotel provoke an uncomfortable anxiety much like following Erwan and his friend through the dark Semenaus house. The exterior of the house is never shown in full, framed to emphasise its holding of secrets. Through the eyes of Erwan, it is a source of fascination, especially the glimpses of the woman at the window. Though the film is set in Paris, a romantic honeymoon destination for Shane and June, there is little of the city's signature beauty on show. In a much later interview, Denis commented that 'I hate seeing a Paris that is just abstractly French' (in Nayman 2009). Notre Dame is one location that is unmistakably Parisian, a tourist destination which encourages June and Shane to perform their role as newlyweds in the city of romance. This is especially important for Shane as his life has become an act, his marriage part of the mask hiding his true murderous self.

Many of the interiors in *Trouble Every Day* – the plane, the hotel and the lab – are generic, almost oppressively so. They align with what Marc Augé (1995) calls non-places, sites of transition defined by solitude and similitude. Augé argues that these locations have developed in response to the increasing movement of people, designed to be passed through, where there is a certain level of anonymity. The plane and hotel are clear example of non-places, sites that people inhabit temporarily and which tend to have very little individuality. The generic sameness they convey creates a sense of familiarity and safety, dampening the anxiety produced by travel and new places. As the hotel was the crux of Denis' initial concept, the connecting thread in her and Assayas' idea for a portmanteau film, this disconcerting feeling of being in a foreign place was always central to the atmosphere of *Trouble Every Day*. June attempts to add a sense of personality to the hotel room by draping the bedside lamp in a scarf featuring the *Mona Lisa*, presumably a souvenir purchased at the Louvre. Yet, this image is so universal that it transcends its connection to Paris and, with the curtains drawn, the room could be anywhere. The research lab is another type of standardised site and we visit several in the film, their interiors filled with white and metal surfaces and industrious machines. However, the lab is not a non-place as it is defined by its purpose rather than its inhabitants, designed for activity and not the comfort of those who perform it.

What connects the interior spaces that appear throughout *Trouble Every Day* is the way they seal characters off from the outside world. Closed windows, unfolded shutters, locked doors, the boarded up bedroom and the plastic screen in the greenhouse lab all create tangible distinctions between inside and outside, as well as insiders and outsiders. When the spaces in the film are accessible – the empty fields, the locker room, Coré's bedroom – and this separation is denied, terrible things happen. However, there is a location in the film that breaches the divide between inside and outside: the balcony. An in-between space, the balcony collapses the boundary between private and public, architecture that contains but also releases the characters. It is a device that reinforces the idea that Shane is emotionally on the edge, teetering between his current life and the dark urges that would untether him from it. When he stands on the hotel balcony alone at night, he might be jetlagged or, more dangerously, plagued by bloody visions (Fig. 21). At Notre-Dame, Shane's time on the balcony with June is a performance, both mimicking horror cinema history as well as his role as a husband on honeymoon. He is

Fig. 21

only shown outside, with the menacing visions of damnation, and not inside the sacred space, where redemption is possible.

The overall palette of the film is subdued, so stronger colours stand out when they are used. Shot in winter, the exterior scenes feature cloudy skies and thin light, overwhelmingly grey and permeated by coldness. Two scenes of the city at dawn, warmed by shades of pink and purple as the sky lightens, at the very start and again towards the end of the film, are fleeting moments of beauty. The sets are largely unobtrusive and nondescript. The lab is a functional space, dominated by white and metal surfaces. The service area of the hotel is similarly about utility rather than appearance, though it appears poorly maintained, with peeling paint, old lockers and visible pipes. The hotel room is an expensive type of generic, styled in complementary shades of apricot, pink and cream in a variety of weighted stripes, including the wallpaper, curtains, carpet, bedspread and bedhead. June's clothes are a notable source of colour, the most memorable being her vibrant emerald green scarf, so sheer it slips away and flies across the city. In the final scene, she wears matching red gloves, shoes and handbag, a colour that ties to the blood on the shower curtain and also recalls Shane's vision of her wrapped in the blood-soaked sheet. Real blood, bright red and viscous, appears throughout the film: in Shane's fantasy, in the fields, painted on the walls, coating bodies. There are also two instances where colour changes are prompted by a change in film stock: over-saturated hues lit by bright fluorescent lights in Shane's memory of his conversation with the red-haired woman and cool, desaturated handheld footage of the misty jungle. Lighting also affects the colour of the scenes, with several filmed in the dark. Lying in their hotel bed at night, Shane and June are bathed in shades of blue and green, their skin warm against the cold white sheets. They are tucked away in their own private world. When Shane stands out on the narrow hotel balcony he is lit by an eerie yellow-green light, conveying a sense of strangeness, both for him, suffering insomnia in a city where he used to live but is no longer home, and for the viewer.

The sound design in *Trouble Every Day* plays an important role in establishing a sense of place, situating the viewer in the narrative world. The music score by Tindersticks melds together a soothing but mournful melody which guides the mood. It is primarily instrumental, dominated by piano and strings. The theme song is the only place with Stuart Staples' vocals, playing in the opening and again in a different arrangement over the credits. The lyrics express the idea of things that are unspoken, repeating 'Look into my eyes / Hear the words I can't say'. Coré and Léo's relationship comes to mind, which is almost completely wordless, expressed through non-verbal communication. The line 'I get on the inside of you' is the closest thing to conveying the heart of the film: the pursuit of complete consummation. The theme song arose from conversations Staples had with Denis before she wrote the screenplay, which she gave to the band to read once completed. Staples explains that she conveyed a feeling of romance that was not necessarily obvious in the text, explaining that what she was really interested in was kissing, why lovers want to bite each other (Anderson 2002; Fischer 2016). Yet, the music conveys a sense of romance that the visuals often do not, continuing when it feels like it should stop. This disjointedness is particularly noticeable in the scene between Coré and Erwan. Commencing as they begin to have sex, the romance of the music conveys their mutual lust, equally desperate for each other. It swells as Coré starts to bite and continues even as she takes it too far, progressing to mutilation. The soft, almost lulling music, with strings and soft percussion, is overwhelmed by their screams, sobs, growls and giggles, making the interaction more excruciating. It ends after the brief cut to Shane so that Erwan takes his final breaths in silence. The soundtrack does not soften the violence as much as emphasise the enduring sadness that follows. Not only is the death of Erwan tragic but it also marks Coré's continuing distance from humanity.

With its gap-filled narrative, the diegetic sound in *Trouble Every Day* becomes especially important. Slightly-augmented ambient noises locate the scenes, such as the distinct clinking of cups and saucers being stacked off-screen at the bar where Shane drinks coffee waiting for Malecot, who raps on the window. The lab equipment is a notable example, with the clicking of glass, sloshing of liquids and mechanical whirring almost overwhelming the various lab scenes. This signals productivity and also, more subtly, the apparent distance and objectivity of science, where machines are tasked with working to provide impartial and undisputable facts. Yet, this research is not infallible. It does nothing to help Coré or Shane, who take medication in the hopes of improving the condition they share, a disease that defies science and, more personally, them as its creators. Another dominant sound repeated in several scenes is the clicking wheels of Christelle's trolley, which tracks her movements through the hotel. It becomes a reminder of the toil and also drudgery of her job, one defined by constant repetition. An aural companion to the shots following the nape of her neck, this sound positions the viewer in her space, becoming a witness to her life and also death.

The film has a noticeable, sometimes frustrating, lack of dialogue, with long stretches without any spoken words. The first line spoken is not until 7.5 minutes into the film and there is a total of only 34 words spoken by the 15 minute mark. In each of the horrific murder scenes, of Erwan and Christelle, there is around 8.5 minutes without dialogue, an exceptionally long time for viewers, who are forced to focus on the terrible activity on screen, punctuated only by screams. Minimal dialogue is a feature across Denis' films. If a scene can be understood without dialogue, she tends to remove it, believing sometimes there is no need for words: 'The type of story I like to tell is another sort of dialogue – it's the dialogue between sound and movement, and feelings and emotion' (in Cochrane 2009). Coré only has one line in the entire film, which is made especially poignant as it is excruciatingly forthright: 'I don't want to wait anymore, Léo. I want to die'. This is also the only verbal exchange between the couple, whose relationship is expressed through gestures. Léo caresses, kisses and bathes Coré, who in return, lets him care for her. She is childlike in her submission and also in her frustration at being locked up and her lack of impulse control. Coré has moved beyond language, she has regressed to having no need for words, conveying everything in her gaze and behaviour. Her need to express herself peaks in the grotesque art she paints in blood across the walls of her house, a tangible, bodily articulation of her desire, which originates from somewhere primal.

HAPTIC CONTACT: INSIDE/OUTSIDE THE NARRATIVE WORLD

The viewer's relationship with the world of *Trouble Every Day* and its characters is slippery and unreliable, defined by a constant sense of unease which builds and never resolves. In a review for *Les Echos*, Danel (2001) describes being at the edge of two worlds, between normality and madness, fantasy and realism, nightmare and reality, sleep and waking. This tenuous state aligns the viewer with Shane, who spends most of the film on a verge – he is plagued by insomnia, ignoring his reveries, refusing to give in to his biology. It is never clear what to believe, with the elliptical plot and camera angles connecting us to the characters in a way that makes it difficult to escape their subjectivity. Looping in and out of the filmic world, we continually cross the same border between inside and outside that Shane and, to an extent, and Coré inhabit. Denis considers this division through the way these two characters appear to and actually interact with the world. Having proved that she will not live by societal rules, Coré is physically separated from the world, locked away. In Paris, Shane and June reside on the border as foreigners, staying temporarily in a hotel, though Shane had lived there in the past so has some familiarity with the city. However, a more pressing dislocation is present in Shane's slowly eroding connection to the social world. He demonstrates the film is not just about having a position on the border but overcoming it, of finding a place, of working out how to exist in the world. For Shane, this means eventually leaning into his urges which, we assume, he intends to incorporate into his life in America. June has already proven an ideal vehicle to support this dual identity, with the honeymoon a façade for his search for Léo. As a devoted wife, she can offer the appearance of a wholesome domestic life that allows, perhaps even covers, for her husband's murderous nocturnal activities. June further promises to function as an anchor to the world, much like Léo tried to be for Coré, not just a means but also a reason to keep searching for a cure. So, Shane will presumably continue to pursue other victims to spare her. But will June let him? And will he be able to stop himself from enacting his fantasy, especially if she confronts him?

Throughout *Trouble Every Day*, the camera both pulls us into and separates us from the narrative. Godard says that when filming 'I always try to make the camera disappear, so that there's nothing in the way between the image and the audience' (in Talu 2018). She draws us uncomfortably close into the story, with repeated close-ups positioning us as voyeurs. Inserted into private spaces where we should not be – the hotel room, a bath, a bedroom, even the lab – we are unseen and, presumably, unwanted. We do not want to be so near the narrative, to follow the characters so closely, seeking a distance that the camera refuses. While some critics feel the film is cold and difficult to connect to, it is arguably the very opposite, too intimate and involving. We are constantly positioned overly near the characters, like at the nape of Christelle's neck or Erwan's face as he is mauled by Coré. This is a likely reason why some people dislike the film so intensely – it involves them too deeply in something enigmatic and never fully explained. But we are too much in the story to get more detailed context. As much as Denis strips everything back, she hints, offers clues and forces us to piece together what we can. She insists 'I am not trying to make it difficult but I think, as a spectator, when I see a movie one block leads me to another block of inner emotion, I think that's cinema. That's an encounter' (in Romney 2000).

The act of looking is central to the reciprocal encounter between viewer and screen in *Trouble Every Day*. Eyes direct the narrative: Coré seduces with her gaze; Léo's eyes are often averted, even physically screened by his helmet visor, avoiding what he needs to realise; June is wide-eyed with confusion and worry (Fig. 22); Shane stares at his intended prey and also repeatedly closes his eyes as he rubs them, tired but also presumably trying to push away the images of his fantasies. Scenes where we intersect the gazes of the characters who are themselves looking amplify the sense of intrusion, that we are seeing something we should not be. The act of looking is especially notable when Erwan discovers Coré (Fig. 23). Appearing behind a door frame that has been hastily boarded up, visible only through the gaps, she stares out at him. Her seduction is wordless. Compelled by her appearance, her fingers reaching through the gap, Erwan needs to interact, to toucher her, to have more. Ripping out the planks by hand, he is desperate to cross the divide between them, to close the gap generated by all the time he watched her window through his own. His urge to consumate is matched by Coré's, who welcomes the lust of the young man – it feeds her own. The camera alternates

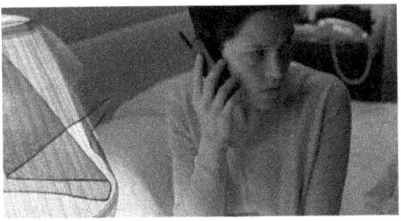 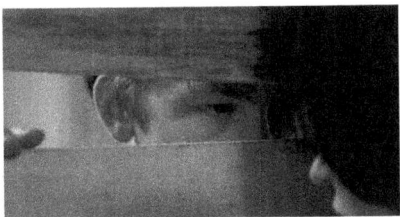

Figs. 22 & 23

between each side of the barrier, her gaze and his. Immersing us in the scene, which we know will end badly for one of them, this heightens our anticipation. The divide reminds us of the danger Coré poses, like a caged animal about to be let loose. We are alternately inside and outside until the boards are pulled down and we are all in the same space, however much we do not want to be.

The idea of borders is epitomised by the relationship between the camera and the window in this film. This is a device that emphasizes the division, but also connection, between inside and outside. As the characters are seen through, and also themselves look through, windows, the viewer is simultaneously separated from and also positioned alongside them. June and Shane are introduced through a window, their heads touching as they look out from the plane taking them to Paris. In their next scene together when they arrive at the hotel, June looks through the back window of the taxi then, from her point of view, Shane returns her smile. When he is at the front desk, she stands outside looking around at her new surrounds, framed by the hotel door, implying a distance between the couple is already starting (Fig. 24). When visiting Jeanne, June waits at the window of her study; rather than being observed, unaware, she is now actively looking, as she searches for answers about Shane's strange behaviour. Shane is also watched through windows: in the aerial shot showing him leaving the lab, when Malecot taps on the café window and as he passes by the camera in a taxi on his way to find Coré. Unlike Coré's first victim in the film, the truck driver who slows down to stare through his window, Shane is wary of what he might find. These moments of separation from Shane are, frankly, a relief, distancing him as his behaviour becomes increasingly terrifying, reflected in the close-ups of his face.

Fig. 24

Early in the film, a striking shot of Coré evokes the iconic image of the woman at the window (see Fig. 5). Seen through a small barred window, she strokes the glass, her touch activating a haptic experience. Her fingers caress the glass like skin, portentous of the sexual activity to come. The woman at the window is a convention familiar from films as varied as British period dramas and Italian gialli. It positions women inside the domestic realm, separated from the outside world physically and symbolically. Framed by the architectural border, Coré is looking but also being looked at. Yet, Erwan is also frequently shown at the window of his bedroom across the road from Coré, with this framing linking them, two people in the suburbs yearning to escape. The glass creates an interface that binds them in their shared fate. Preceding the image of Coré, Erwan is introduced leaning out his window, seen from below, watching the Semeneaus' house. This is immediately followed by a shot of Léo looking out their bedroom window before closing the shutters and fastening a heavy bar, blocking Erwan's prying gaze. There is a triangular relationship between these characters – Erwan is as curious about Léo as he is Coré, where he goes during his strict schedule and what he is doing in the house. When the teen eventually decides to go inside, his breaking of the window fractures this divide.

The closeness between the camera, characters and viewer, between image and sensation, is at the forefront of *Trouble Every Day*. Godard remarks that she engenders this while working, explaining 'what often happens to me when I'm filming is to be so close to things as to feel like I'm almost touching them. It's very haptic and maybe a form of eroticism too' (in Talu 2018). Through their effort to dissolve the barrier between image and viewer, Godard and Denis work together to fashion a tactile gaze, allowing viewers to feel not just as close to the action as they are, but more so. For example, when Shane and June are in bed, their bodies entwined, the viewer is not just in front of the skin but on the skin. By engaging the viewer through the sense of touch, *Trouble Every Day* enacts Laura U. Marks' (2000) theory of haptic visuality. Marks argues that films do not just invite identification but encourage a bodily relationship between viewer and image. Haptic images appeal not only to sight and sound but to all the senses, encouraging the viewer to relinquish any sense of separateness from the image. Vivian Sobchack (2004) maintains that embodied spectatorship opens a film beyond its visible containment by the screen, describing, for instance, how it might affect the body, sensitising the skin or constricting the chest. Alongside such phenomenological arguments, there are data-driven studies that measure physiological responses to cinema, especially the horror genre. These are not just limited to visible expressions, such as screaming, grimacing, jumping, crying or shutting the eyes, but can also be measured in increases in heart rate, blood pressure and skin temperature. Such physical changes connect the viewer to the characters, creating an identification that is not bound just to the narrative but, more deeply, to their bodies. While there is, like Godard said, something erotic about this intimacy, it is certainly not always enjoyable. In *Trouble Every Day*, it provokes more ambivalent feelings, including anxiety, frustration and revulsion. Denis explains that with *Trouble Every Day*, she was thinking about phrases which describe physical states of the body, like 'avoir quelqu'un dans la peau' (having someone in the skin), which means to be mad about and 'pleurer des larmes de sang' (crying tears of blood), to suffer the agony of remorse or disappointment (in Creutz 2001). She wants us to experience the world of her characters not only in a conceptual but a corporeal way.

One of the most haptic sequences in *Trouble Every Day* is Shane's fantasy of June draped in a blood-soaked sheet. The camera roams across her body, its nakedness accentuated by the wet fabric which is so heavy with blood it cannot absorb any more. This overflow is uncomfortably tactile, with a palpable feeling of oozing fabric sticking to wet skin. Skin, fabric and blood become one mass, the textures merging together. The folds of the material are gathered in a way that evokes rumpled bedding from a sexual scenario but made wrong. The excess of blood represents the breaking of the barrier between inside and outside – the inside cannot be contained. In the overwhelming blackness of the surrounds, evoking the drama of Baroque painting, the senses are heightened, emitting a feeling of heat and a metallic scent. In the way June yields to the bloodied sheet there is also an echo of the legend of Elizabeth Bathory, the Hungarian countess who apparently bathed in the blood of her victims. But it is unclear if June is the victim, if the blood is her own, or if it is that of another – a victim of Shane's, or maybe even her own? It is, of course, Shane's dream, but it is unclear in what way he will incorporate June into his activities, if he will share his darkest fantasies with her.

BAROQUE, ROCOCO AND SURFACE

Trouble Every Day evokes the Baroque tradition in both its aesthetic and its preoccupation with surfaces, the body and sensual – often violent – contact. Established at the end of the sixteenth century in Rome, Baroque art spread across Western Europe and persisted well into the eighteenth century. From its initial religious subject matter, commissioned by the Catholic Church, the style was imitated by artists in royal courts, notably in France and Spain, seeking to align with the Vatican. Then, further north in Protestant countries like Holland, it was adapted by artists producing a new type of secular work for the homes of the recently wealthy merchant classes. The Baroque is defined by a sense of theatricality, movement and extreme realism, intending to rouse the senses of the viewer, whether a Caravaggio biblical painting, a Diego Velázquez portrait or a Frans Hals still life. Denis draws from its use of realism to evoke sensations, especially in the representation of skin. As Baroque artists mimetically transformed their canvas (or stone) into skin, Denis does the same with the screen. Indeed, Nancy (2001) argues that *Trouble Every Day* is filmed entirely on and about the skin, playing with the word *pellicula*, the French word for both surfaces. It films nothing else but skin, he contends, so much so that it confuses the two, with the image itself torn into a wound. The confusion of skin and screen, of real and fictive bodies, draws viewers into the narrative space of the film, where they inhabit the same world as the characters. This is reminiscent of how Baroque art employs compositional techniques like foreshortening and tenebrism to invite viewers into its space, disturbing the division between them and the image. The breakdown of the physical barrier posed by the canvas or camera lens is certainly evident in *Trouble Every Day*, where the line between the space of the characters and viewers dissolves.

In a discussion of the connection between *Trouble Every Day* and the Baroque, Saige Walton (2013) turns to Gilles Deleuze's notion of the fold. Deleuze argues that the Baroque creates infinite folds which twist and layer across time and space, a body of surfaces that couples abstract form with sensation. Walton persuasively argues that *Trouble Every Day* enacts a Neo-Baroque texturing of sensation, enfolding images and sounds in a way that defies the presumed flatness of the screen. She also considers the technical aspects of Baroque art, particularly its focus on the mastery of highly textural illusions, such as in Bernini's agitated drapery and Caravaggio's painting of bloodied wounds. It is these art historical references in *Trouble Every Day* that are of especial interest here, part of a broader program of references in the film (discussed further in chapter 4).

Trouble Every Day is indebted to the formal elements of the Baroque, like colour, space and line, as well as its subject matter. The film also evokes the sense of exaggeration and also violence imbued in much Baroque art, both narratively and stylistically. Its aggressively embellished canvases and sculptures convey physical and emotional tautness. Denis utilises negative space to emphasise drama. The characters are frequently set against deep black backgrounds: Léo in the field, June in Shane's fantasy, Shane in the Semeneau house and Coré in her bedroom. Many scenes shot almost in darkness evoke a Baroque aesthetic, with chiaroscuro taken to the extreme. However, this dramatic contrast of light and dark is used to obscure rather than highlight what is being shown. For instance, the images of Shane lurking in the shadows of Coré's house and again in the hotel waiting for Christelle, his face barely emerging from the completely black background, are studies in tenebrism. Shane's face is repeatedly framed against a background free of extraneous details, often buried in darkness, evoking the drama of Caravaggio (Fig. 25). For instance, in three versions of *David with the Head of Goliath* (c.1599, c.1607 and c.1606-1610), the giant's dark curly hair frames a mouth frozen in a final silent scream. Echoing this agony, Shane is overcome by emotional turmoil, which, it seems, manifests as a physical pain. He is defeated by a force he could never have predicted. Caravaggio's use of chiaroscuro creates a drama that is centred on the scene, with the deliberately bare background offering nowhere for the eye to wander. Similarly, Denis offers little respite from Shane's troubled and, increasingly, troubling, gaze.

Fig. 25

Baroque art is obsessed with the corporeal, where everything is heightened: tense muscles, askew limbs and tactile skin. The lack of distance from pictorial bodies is especially affective with distressing, even gruesome, subjects, like the horror of Artemisia Gentileschi's *Judith Beheading Holofernes* (1610), her first version of this biblical story. The way that the artist flattens the picture plane, positioning the viewer too close to the horror with nowhere to go in this gruesome scene, brings to mind the scene of Coré murdering Erwan. There is a deep sense of brutality in both, though of course Judith is deliberate and rational as opposed to Coré, who is taken over by instinct. The way that Denis manipulates the emotions of the viewer through the representation of body – in this case, Erwan's – echoes Gentileschi's exceptionally realistic portrayal of the murder; the pained face of Holofernes; the taut arms of the maidservant holding him down, the blood dripping down the sheet. The emphasis on flesh, on skin and touch, is also noticeable in the work of the Flemish Baroque artist Peter Paul Rubens. In *Massacre of the Innocents* (1611-12), a mass of bodies, intertwined torsos, limbs and fabric, is pushed towards the viewer. Again, there is no distance from the horrific narrative but, unlike Gentileschi's pared-back scene, the image is overflowing with details. The exaggerated attention to the surface renders the different textures – skin, cloth, stone – the same, creating one tactile volume. Drawing the viewer into the sensuous paintwork forces them to engage with the subject but its very beauty also creates a sense of remove.

The emphasis on surface became even more pronounced in the Rococo, a movement which flourished in eighteenth-century France. Emerging from the Baroque, Rococo art applied the style devised to exalt religion to secular subjects, like mythology, love and leisure. The turn to thematically and visually playful art and design reminded contemporary viewers of their lives, of the sensual pleasures of the court. The Rococo encourages viewers to luxuriate in textures: when looking at François Boucher's *The Toilette of Venus* (1751), for example, we can feel the coolness of flesh, thick velvet, heavy folds of silk, smooth pearls. But illusionism is less important than conveying an overall atmosphere, with a sense of fantasy pervading the art. Yet, realism is still important, especially in design elements such as illusionistic wall and ceiling panels painted to look like real places, like gardens or the sky, tying two-dimensional images into the real world. Lavish Rococo surfaces forge immersive worlds which viewers do not just imagine touching but actually being in. In Fragonard's *The Swing* (1767), the thick ruffled layers of the dress and petticoats are palpable as they swish with the momentum of the swing. We at once feel the vertiginous thrill of being airborne – its unconcealed allegory for sexual intercourse – and the voyeurism of the man watching the woman. The painting demonstrates how fictive subjects are subsumed into their environments – skin blends into fabric, fabric into foliage, foliage into clouds. The way that the layering of textures in Rococo art overwhelms the viewer, aligning them with the subjects in the work, echoes haptic cinema. It precedes Sobchack's argument about embodied spectatorship in film, creating an exchange between viewer and image. As much as Denis' images visually align with the realism of the Italian Baroque, the reciprocity forged by its descendent, the Rococo, with its obsession with surfaces, is just as important. *Trouble Every Day* is obsessed with touch, not in just mimetic way but a more broad all-encompassing way.

The interest in surfaces, both physical and symbolic, in *Trouble Every Day* is reflected in the relationship between clothing and the body. Clothes both separate and contain the body, distinguishing between inside and outside. They also say something of the wearer.

Fig. 26

June's layers of tailored clothing cover almost all her skin when she is in public, the thick fabric of her buttoned-up suits conveying a demure conservativeness. There is something very old-fashioned and overly demure about packing these matching skirts and jackets as a honeymoon wardrobe, aligning June with ingénues from mid-twentieth-century cinema. Yet, when she is not fully-dressed she is completely naked, in the privacy of her room. Coré dresses in very little – a thin black slip, a sheer white nightdress, a silky robe – conveying an overt sexiness which is an obvious contrast to June (Fig. 26). The oversized coat, a necessity she dons when going out in the cold, emphasises the alluring thinness of the slip beneath and the bare skin of her legs. Its bulk creates a deceptive sense of smallness and vulnerability. Christelle, meanwhile, wears a uniform while at the hotel, a shapeless square button down tunic with a knee length hem and elbows to the sleeves, in bland grey and white stripes. Featureless and unobtrusive, this outfit is designed to draw attention away from the wearer, making her blend into the hotel interior. Yet, she is shown getting dressed and undressed, a reminder that this uniform is temporary and not representative of her, just her job. When arriving at and leaving work on the back of a motorbike, Christelle wears a leather jacket and a purple scarf. These brief scenes offer a small glimpse of her life outside the hotel, which we know little about.

ABJECTION AND THE BODY UNDONE

Julia Kristeva's theory of abjection offers a post-structural framework for an analysis of the representation of the body and its connection to the relationship between inside and outside in *Trouble Every Day*. In *Powers of Horror* (1982), Kristeva argues that the abject is the place where meaning collapses, disturbing identity, systems and order with no respect for borders, positions and rules. It is represented in bodily fluids, like blood, urine, excrement, which are revolting because they remind us of mortality (though Kristeva does not consider tears and sperm as polluting, although they belong to borders of the body). Blood features in *Trouble Every Day*, of course, released from and coating bodies. There is also a focus on cleanliness throughout the film, with the maids' daily repetition of their tasks to keep the hotel maintained. Christelle is shown cleaning the bathroom in the Browns' room, a reminder of how the body expels pollutants, and the need for these to be scrubbed away, physically and symbolically. The abject is also present in the close-ups of brains. Removed from the body, sliced into segments, the former receptacle of identity, an individual's sense of self, is reduced to meat. Kristeva argues that selfhood is intimately bound up with the constitution of a sense of stable subjectivity, coherent speech, and the clean and proper body. In defying each of these things, Coré embodies abjection.

Coré's behaviour enacts the collapse of boundaries between inside and outside that Kristeva positions as a cause of abjection. When she penetrates the body, ripping men apart to leave behind bloodied corpses, she crosses a physical boundary as well as a social one. The moment where Coré pokes her finger into the dying Erwan's open cheek exemplifies taking the curious lust-fuelled exploration of the body during sex to the extreme. Pushing through the muscle and fat and, of course, blood, she treats him not like a human at all. She desires what is below it, she wants more. Like Stuart Staples intones in the theme song from the introduction, 'I get on the inside of you'. Of filming this scene, Denis told Nancy 'then there was the first bite – even when you read it in the script there was the feeling that we were trespassing, going over a forbidden line, and I believe I was not the only one who felt that way' (in Vecchio 2014). Shane similarly dehumanises Christelle when he rapes her and then eats her. By crossing the physical border of the body, piercing skin through their teeth, Coré and Shane sever their connection to humanity. Whatever disease they share, it strips away what makes them human. The way that they both treat the bodies of their victims like flesh, or, more so, like meat, is a horrifying reminder that humans are fragile, that skin is only a thin layer that protects all the things inside. Their transgressions contravene all social and moral codes. By showing these horrendous situations, Denis reflects on these limits, on what it means to be human. She says, 'it seemed to me necessary to go on the fringes that are those of the present time: not to show the scenes of devoration is what would have been, for me, inadmissible' (in Frodon 2001).

The horror genre is closely tied to the abject, with its preponderance of corpses – the utmost image of abjection – and blood. The three dead bodies we see are grotesque, blood and wounded flesh prompting sense of physical revulsion. Fargeau says that when writing *Trouble Every Day*, he and Denis looked at the way blockbusters had made gore acceptable in the cinema (in Gibbons and Jeffries 2001). Drawing from Kristeva, Barbara Creed (1993) explores abjection in horror films as expressed in the female body. Creed argues that despite how it might seem, women are not just victims in the genre but that the female reproductive body is actually the source of horror. While Coré does not neatly fit into one of Creed's categories of monstrous-feminine, she embodies many of its characteristics. She visualises how close-up shots of gaping jaws, sharp teeth and bloodied lips play on the spectators' fears of bloody incorporation. She exists on the wrong side of the border which separates the living from that which threatens its extinction.

The treatment of bodies in horror films is part of a broader connection between sex and violence in the genre, where naked flesh is exposed only to be mutilated and both characters and viewers are titillated and punished for looking. In *Trouble Every Day*, this is taken to the extreme. The close-ups of fragmented body parts align Denis and Godard's approach to filming bodies with pornography. Godard even explains that she 'treated the gory scenes as sex scenes' (in Vié 2002). In her discussion of body genres, Linda Williams (1991) argues that pornography, melodrama and horror are genres that treat women and bodies in the same way, featuring gratuitous bodily excesses. She argues that these sensations are visually expressed in bodily fluids: ejaculation, blood and tears in pornography, horror and melodrama, respectively. Each of these is in evidence in *Trouble Every Day*, and, further, can be aligned with three characters: Coré with blood, which she extracts and then paints with; June with tears, crying inside and outside the hotel; and Shane, who ejaculates across the bathroom mirror. These fluids, of course, also engage with abjection, polluting the world around them, crossing the border between inside and outside. They also remind us of the violence, both emotional and physical, that weaves through the film.

Desire is violence: Kissing, biting, eating

Trouble Every Day is about desire taken to the extreme. It is a condition that grows and transforms, takes hold, takes over and destroys. The narrative world is disturbed by the manifestation of violent inner fantasies, where terrible urges are enacted to disastrous results. Denis suggests that it is through the libido that we become aware of the terrible urges that lurk inside us all (in Bonnaud 2001). The feelings that the film taps into are so dangerous they should be kept inside, imagined, restrained by reason and social rules. When Coré and Shane ignore this expectation they disturb the social order, with their terrible actions severing their ties to humanity. In the documentary *Claire Denis, The Vagabond* (1996), the director remarks 'I'm interested in the slice of humanity that surrounds a monster'. In *Trouble Every Day*, Denis documents the way that this slice thins by contrasting Shane to Coré, who has progressed further in her monstrosity, has slipped further away from what it means to be human. Both characters reflect Denis' belief in the ambiguity of what defines evil, an idea that threads throughout her films. She tells Frodon (2001) that *Trouble Every Day* opposes the idea, common to so many films, that the evil is external, carried by others, the 'bad guys'. Coré and Shane represent the constantly pressing question of who is the danger, who is the enemy. Neither seems like an obvious risk, with the threat they present concealed by other factors. For Coré, this is her beauty and seductive femininity and for Shane, his career and marriage. Yet, both have unspeakable desires so overwhelming that they rupture into the real world, endangering everyone in their radius.

Expressed as a physical hunger, desire in *Trouble Every Day* becomes all-consuming: kissing progresses to biting then to eating. At the press conference at Cannes, Denis explained that the film is about how close the kiss is to the bite. She described it as a love story and, more specifically, referenced a mother's love, recalling a childhood dream in which her mother tucked her in and devoured her with kisses, suggesting that every mother wants to eat her baby with love. Indeed, the kiss that turns into a bite is the central motif of the film. Established in the opening scene, this idea intensifies throughout the film. Shane's kisses along the inside of June's arm lead to a bite mark on her shoulder and later another on her lip, which progress to his frenzied eating of Christelle. The bite on June's arm (we can assume there are more) is a promise, but of what we do not know (Fig. 27). Is it that he will always stop himself with her, pulling back when he wants to go further? Or does it mark her for death, a sign that, eventually, he will keep going, his teeth breaking through skin. Nancy (2001) explores *Trouble Every Day* through this image of the bite mark, which he calls the *icône de l'acharnement*, which translates to icon of fury or relentlessness. Through his philosophical lens, Nancy argues that kissing is a kind of devouring, that the kiss mingles souls and the bite explodes the soul.

Fig. 27

The image of the mouth which recurs throughout *Trouble Every Day* is not just about kissing, biting and eating but also, of course, about expressing sound. As noted earlier, Coré has little need for words anymore, expressing herself in a non-verbal language: she emits a disturbing combination of girlish giggles and animalistic grunts and growls. Yet, the men she is with seem to not care. The mouth is also a tool for screaming, which is especially important in horror films. Close-ups of a woman with her mouth open wide shrieking in terror are a staple in the genre, featuring in films as varied as *King Kong* (Cooper, Schoedsack, 1933), *Psycho* (Hitchcock, 1960), *Texas Chain Saw Massacre* (Hooper, 1974), *Suspiria*, *The Shining*, *Possession* (Zulawski, 1980), *Scream* (Craven, 1996) and *Hereditary* (Aster, 2018). In *Trouble Every Day*, Christelle's face – filmed upside down, her mouth open as she screams while trying to fight Shane off – is a familiar image, though more distressing than most, less exaggerated and more realistic. The power of the scream is most apparent when the woman is silenced. Screaming in terror is, of course, closely aligned with screaming in pleasure, both visually and aurally, with close-ups of the faces of dying women in horror filmed like orgasms in pornography, which again brings to mind Williams' connection between the genres. This confusion is particularly evident in vampire films. When the woman's neck is exposed, penetrated by fangs, she tends to swoon, woozy and sometimes overtly experiencing pleasure. Often, she is pulled under the spell of the vampire, willingly submitting to his needs, and often her death.

The connection between sex and violence dominates *Trouble Every Day*, a theme which manifests throughout Denis' work: 'I think sexuality isn't gentle, nor is desire. Desire is violence' (in Darke 2000). This relationship is typical in horror cinema, bound together and taken to the extreme in the two gruesome on-screen murders in the film. Denis explains that her interest in making a genre film was because of its relationship to sensuality and sexuality (in Harrer 2001a). Yet, she also points out that she is not interested in sex between characters but rather 'the sexual charge that passes between the actors and the spectators' (in Darke 2000). If this is the aim, then viewers are not just observers but rather participants in the horrible acts of violence that are tied to sex here, complicit and perhaps even responsible for the frisson that prompts them. Yet, Dalle describes the film as 'very violent and not just because of the murders' (in Péron 2000). There is an underlying ferocity to the emotions in *Trouble Every Day*, such as the way that Léo loves Coré so much that he keeps her close, trying to cure her and covering-up her murders, or Coré's choice to die rather than continue this destructive life. Shane seems endlessly stressed about his urges, with his love for June making him worried that he will enact his fantasies with her and so kill her. Both men are protective towards their wives, yet the women have their own ideas about how they will live and thwart these plans with their autonomous decisions.

While *Trouble Every Day* is very much about desire, it is also about connection, about the physical and emotional ties that define the lives of the characters and, more importantly, what it means to be human. The narrative is shaped by the idea of love as much as lust. In particular, the honeymoon scenario reminds us of the gravity of the decision by two people to spend a lifetime together, with June radiating with the optimism and adoration of new love, at least at the start of the film. The seriousness of these vows are taken to the extreme by Léo as he cares for Coré, hiding her away and keeping her condition, and her crimes, secret. There is a suggestion in the film that marriage changes the nature and also expression of desire. Shane wants to consume his wife, but, once married, he seems to have vowed to protect her from himself. This means he has to pursue other women to not hurt her. Like Coré's affairs, it is cheating nonetheless. But how do they not kill their spouses? There must be some level of self-control. Is their love imprinted on them in a way, their vows inscribed on their skin? Or is it the relationships themselves that influence their condition – is it Shane's recent marriage that hastens the changes in his behaviour? Does the very thing he thinks will save him actually push him towards a permanent psychic disintegration, and instead of binding him into the social fabric further degrade this link? Coré and Shanes still seek connection with their spouses, whether this is a positive thing or not, reminding us that intimacy is not only physical but also emotional. For Coré, these seem to be separate, suggesting again that she is further down the path of devolution, able to, or maybe forced to, sever the corporal from the psychological, physical touch from connection, lust from love.

Trouble Every Day questions the very nature of desire. As scientists, Coré, Léo and Shane are interested in its biological origin, working to discover more about the libido and how it can be manipulated. They are so invested in the search that they trial the plant they found in Guyana themselves, an illegal, incredibly dangerous and, eventually fatal, decision. Their neurological modification, a field about which very little is understood, disturbs the natural balance. *Trouble Every Day* positions desire *as* disease, something which takes over the body, a biological imperative that cannot be overridden. The brain is changed – perhaps irreversibly – and science cannot control its creation. As a scientist, Léo treats Coré like a patient, trying to understand and control her condition with medication. With his career collapsing after he published his findings, working in the lab in his house becomes his new job and looking after Coré his primary concern. Yet, her behaviour goes against science, against nature, so it follows that she cannot be fixed by it. Similarly, Shane is a researcher who believes that science is the answer, trialling various pharmaceuticals. Yet, he still devolves throughout the film. Coré was also once a scientist, and faith in this work could not save her. Her life, once organised by reason and logic, careful measuring and slow processes, became driven by emotion, without any consideration for rationality or rules. Léo and Shane both search for a cure for, or at least management of, something biological, but their failures suggest they are missing something. They are looking in the wrong place by turning to science, which still does not completely understand the workings of the brain, in response to a problem that is more mysterious, primal and profound. 'The evil question does not have a vaccine,' Denis warns (in Creutz 2001).

There is an underlying question in this film of whether Shane and Coré can actually control their behaviour, override their biology. Shane is obviously fighting his feelings, and so is Coré, sometimes – allowing herself to be locked up, requesting to die, lighting the fire. There is enough humanity left in her to recognise what she is doing is wrong. But she cannot resist her impulses – she throws away her pills, she escapes, she entices Erwan into her room. A related question is, who to blame for their behaviour? While the scientists would have known the risk of human trials, they could not have known that it would create a seemingly irreversible affliction. If they cannot control their actions, can they be held responsible for them? Is it Léo who is accountable for aiding Coré, keeping her condition a secret and covering-up her murders? Will June do things differently when she hears about Christelle, when Shane's behaviour gets increasingly strange or when the murders start in America, as they surely will?

The problem of desire in *Trouble Every Day* is embodied by Coré. As a woman with a libido so strong that she is physically dangerous, she has to be locked up because, she cannot contain her urges. When she escapes, she seduces, murders and eats men. Of course, Shane is also overwhelmed by these feelings, but it is Coré whose condition has progressed further, who has apparently not been able to manage her needs. There is something primal and instinctual in her behaviour that says something about the way women are represented on screen. Coré offers a heightened example of the negative stereotypes of womanhood that are perpetuated in society. She is wild, emotional and reactive, the hysterical woman taken to its extreme. Dangerous when unrestrained, taking no heed of expectations, Coré needs to be controlled. She is locked up, fed drugs, separated from her old life. She is also hyper-sexual, easily seducing men to satisfy herself. Echoing the subtle manipulation of the 1940s femme fatale, Coré engages the disguise of a woman in distress to draw men to her. Coré addresses the tense relationship between women and hunger, both physical and sexual. The act of eating can of course signify many things: nourishment, care, hospitality. Tables laden with a cornucopia of food, as represented in seventeenth-century Dutch still lives, exemplify wealth and indulgence. Eating can also be about gratification, overindulging in an excess that is not necessary but, regardless, enjoyed. An appetite for food can also be seen as a metaphor for sexual desire. Both types of hunger are problematic in representations of women, referring to each other. The idea that women have desires disturbs the idea that they are objects to be filled. Coré represents what can happen if they do not quell their hunger.

In *Trouble Every Day*, cannibalism is a metaphor for excessive, unrestrained desire, a craving for complete incorporation that crosses bodily and social boundaries. Cannibalism exemplifies transgression, a taboo ingrained into the fabric of Western society. The revulsion provoked by the acts of cannibalism in the film taps into a deep horror. The idea of people reduced to their physical qualities, to meat, problematizes the idea that humans are more than that. Cannibalism has been studied across various fields, including anthropology, history, literature, palaeontology and philosophy. The idea of boundaries recurs in discussions about the subject, which distinguish and, more importantly, separate the Other, from the known. In anthropology, cannibalism is divided loosely into two categories: endo- and exo-cannibalism, or eating of people inside and outside the community. Both involve rituals of incorporation; the first in eating the dead as a sign of respect and the latter as a display of power. They are about absorbing something of the individual. However, there are other categories of cannibalism, including survival, sexual, auto and medicinal. Coré is clearly a sexual cannibal, eating people as a form of gratification. Yet, with her biology altered, she also kills because she cannot help it.

Denis distances *Trouble Every Day* from the cannibal subgenre. At the press conference at Cannes, she insisted 'by no means did I want to go as far as cannibalism and going beyond certain limits would not have been modern' (Harrer 2001a). A later comment expands on this, explaining: 'I'm inclined to think that there is something wrong with the cannibal genre. It's either the *Raft of The Medusa* and we eat to not die, which is still rare, or cannibalism is ritual. That being said...it is about the tales of Perrault, paintings by Goya: something that is essentially the desire to satiate a sexual appetite, rather than the urge to eat human flesh' (in Bonnaud 2001). Of course, it is this very connection between cannibalism and sexual desire that is at the very core of *Trouble Every Day*. The desire for flesh leads to sex and then to eating, contravening all rules. Denis mentions the *Raft of The Medusa*, an 1819 painting by Théodore Gericault about a scandalous shipwreck in 1816 where survival cannibalism was practiced by the few people who were rescued after 13 days at sea. She also references Goya, which must be in regards to *Saturn Devouring His Son* (1819-23), a savage mythological murder. *Trouble Every Day* is undeniably more closely aligned with fine art than exploitation cinema. Yet, while Denis might separate her film from a long lineage of cannibals on screen, it certainly taps into this history and, importantly, the ideas that shaped it. *Trouble Every Day* is full of references from cinema, art, photography, literature and folklore, which will be explored in the next chapter.

4. SITUATING THE FILM: REFERENCES AND LINEAGE

Trouble Every Day is replete with visual and narrative references that shape the film while also constantly thwarting attempts to firmly situate it. A diverse range of images are evoked, from classic cinema to Abstract Expressionism. Denis drew inspiration from fairy-tales and fantastic literature, especially the gothic stories of Sheridan Le Fanu. She started with films she loves, like Jean Cocteau's *Beauty and the Beast* (1946) and Jacques Tourneur's *Cat People* (1942), which address the line between human and animal. But she was also inspired by contemporary genre cinema, including films by directors such as Dario Argento, David Cronenberg and Abel Ferrara. *Trouble Every Day* is frequently assessed within the context of the New French Extremity. However, it sits in a much longer lineage of films that push the boundary of taste and representation, designed to shock and repulse. The silent Surrealist film *Un Chien Andalou* (1929) is as much its predecessor as the Italian cannibal exploitation films of the 1970s and 1980s. When *Trouble Every Day* was released, Denis was one of several international filmmakers who committed to provocative displays of violence on screen, part of a broader cinematic movement.

REFERENCES IN *TROUBLE EVERY DAY*

As with many of her films, Denis found inspiration for *Trouble Every Day* in fine art. At the 2001 Cannes press conference, Denis mentioned having seen self-portraits made by Descas, who like Gallo is also an artist, painted in shades of red and orange, representing wounds on his body. She compared the carnal quality of these images, and the colour palette, to paintings Jean-Michel Basquiat: 'They were dark red, which gave an impression of dried blood. I think these sensations served for the rewriting of the film' (in Harrer 2001b). She and Descas had seen these together years earlier at an exhibition in Paris, where they were filming *No Fear, No Die* (1990), images of 'corpses and skeletons with deathlike smiles' which Denis gave him as a reference for how he should shoot the final scene (in Reid 1996). Shades of red continued to preoccupy Denis in *I Can't Sleep*, where the hotel rooms were inspired by a memory of Francis Bacon: 'I wanted to film an image that expressed all those bodies in Bacon's raw, fleshy pictures. I thought that this feeling should pervade my film, which is a story about raw flesh' (in Reid 1996). *Trouble Every Day* is also of course about flesh, but it is literal rather than metaphorical in its treatment of the body. The production design does not need to turn to this palette as there are actual blood and wounds in the story. However, June's final costume features matching red heels, gloves and handbag, a colour that is most striking when she returns to the hotel, a visual parallel to the blood Shane wipes from the shower curtain, except for that one telling drop. June is aligned, almost implicated, in her husband's activities; the question is, what will she do with her knowledge? Will she end up with blood on her hands, like Leo does as he washes Coré? Or will she make a different choice?

Trouble Every Day is indebted to historical art, especially the narrative and visual drama of the Baroque, as discussed in the previous chapter. Its emphasis on naturalism – forgoing manufactured beauty in favour of unidealised images drawn from everyday life – is also reminiscent of nineteenth-century French Realism. In the audio commentary for the scene where Shane masturbates in the bathroom, Denis draws a comparison between his face and a self-portrait by Gustave Courbet, one of the most prominent artists in this movement (Fig. 28). This is *The Desperate Man* (1843-5), a recognisable painting where the artist's face pushes into the foreground, eyes wide in an expression of panic as he tugs his messy long curls through his hands. The exaggerated gesture, highlighted by the contrast between light and dark, echoes the images of Shane throughout the film, whose constant stress is signalled by rubbing his eyes and forehead. Courbet's study of intense emotion aligns with Shane's inner turmoil, though, despite briefly breaking down when he approaches Coré and physically pushing June away, he generally conceals his feelings. However, French Realism is not just about mimesis but using it to capture a subjective experience, an aim which aligns with Denis' approach to filmmaking.

Trouble Every Day also draws from a visual history of images of women bathing, a subject that lends itself to the alluring, often sensual, display of the body. Classical mythology has long offered a justification for creating and exhibiting such images, appropriate when positioned as intellectual objects of history and fine art. The bath of Diana, Roman goddess of the hunt, for instance, was painted by artists such as Titian (c.1556-9), Rembrandt (1634), Rubens (c.1635-40), Watteau (c.1715) and Boucher (1742). In most of these images, women are often joined by attendants to wash them, bathing depicted

Fig. 28

as a communal activity. Coré is similarly washed, but by her husband. In the late-eighteenth century, artists turned their gaze towards more everyday scenes, of women bathing in the privacy of their homes. They might be seen undressing or partially dressed, shown in close-ups of shoulders, breasts and knees. The scene of Christelle washing her feet in the sink after her shift, for example, recalls the work of Pierre Bonnard and Edgar Degas, who repeatedly returned to the subject of women bathing in the late nineteenth and early twentieth centuries. These men sought to convey a sense of realism in their depiction of bodies as well as the impression that these women were unaware of them, attending to their daily activities in private. Degas in particular was known for having his models adopt difficult poses, like Christelle's, often using dancers who had the stamina to hold these. The ease with which Christelle manoeuvres into her awkward position shows this is a repeated practice, part of the routine that fuels her boredom. The scene firmly positions her as working class, unlike the women upstairs in the hotel who soak in the bathtubs she has scrubbed. For instance, June is shown relaxing stretched out in the deep bath, a leisurely activity on holiday – though this mood is disturbed when she opens her eyes to see Shane staring down with his serial-killer eyes. She is rightly startled, momentarily scared as he is in a complete position of power; Janet Leigh in *Psycho* immediately comes to mind. A beautiful woman taking a bath is a familiar scene in the horror genre. Like in art, this is a situation that allows for nudity, which is expected in B-grade offerings. But it can also signal that a character is in danger and, frequently, their pending demise: particularly iconic scenes include *Blood and Black Lace* (Bava, 1964), *The Toolbox Murders* (Donnelly, 1978) and *A Nightmare on Elm Street* (Craven, 1984). These images remind us that bathing can put women in a vulnerable position, where they are not just naked but also trapped in a location from which it is difficult to escape.

Coré's ghastly non-figurative art, painted on the walls of her house in blood, engages with Abstract Expressionism (Fig. 29). Developing in New York in the mid-1940s, art in this movement was bound to the identity of the artist, who sought to tap into a universal experience, to discover primal images and emotions that Coré not only has access to but embodies. In pursuit of this state, Abstract Expressionists followed the Surrealists, inspired by practices like automatic drawing, where artists sought to create without actively thinking, hand guided by their unconscious. Coré echoes this act in her blood-art, the designs emerging while under the influence of her condition, reduced to a primal state. The action paintings of Jackson Pollock are evoked here, with the vertical lines of blood dripping down the walls, amid sweeping arcs and decisive lines. In the cultural imagination, the Abstract Expressionist was a hyper-masculine figure, emblematic of the virile man of post-WWII America. This did not leave much space for the women working in this movement, like Lee Krasner – Pollock's wife – or Helen Frankenthaler, neglect that is slowly being recognised in academic and institutional fields. If these Abstract Expressionist paintings can be understood as an expression of masculinity, a thinly veiled metaphor for ejaculation, Coré takes a decisively feminine approach to her work. By painting straight onto the wall, she takes control of the realm that is supposedly hers – the house – marking the domestic space to which she has been physically relegated. There is also a suggestion of menstruation in her blood-soaked dress, a sign of the dangerous female body. Her use of blood as a medium has a precedent in contemporary art. Women artists such as Judy Chicago, Tracey Emin and Carolee Schneeman have all used menstrual blood in their work. Especially relevant here is Anna Mendieta's performative art of the 1970s and 1980s, which often featured blood. For instance, in *Blood Sign #2* (1974) and *Body Tracks* (1982), the artist coated her hands and arms in a mixture of animal blood and tempera before deliberately dragging them down a sheet of paper, a document of gesture and mark of her presence that is very much like Coré's.

Fig. 29

The aesthetic of *Trouble Every Day* is indebted to the work of Canadian photographer Jeff Wall. Best known for his large-scale images inspired by the tradition of history painting, the artist constructs complex tableaux that resemble still-lives, made tense by their stillness and too-smooth surfaces. Godard explains that after Denis showed her Wall's work, she strove to capture the anxiety they contained: 'They looked pretty banal, nothing spectacular happened in them, but at the same time there was like a deadly menace looming' (in Talu 2018). In particular, the scenes set in between Paris and the suburbs, the unattractive open fields where Coré hunts, evoke Walls work. These are places that people pass through, in-between, slightly removed from daily life. Denis and Godard point to their direct inspiration by Wall several times during the audio commentary: when Léo finds the van empty at the start of the film, Coré at the window, Shane waiting at the lab and the trashed bedroom (Fig. 30). The last example specifically references *The Destroyed Room* (1978), a bedroom in disarray, including a slashed mattress upturned against the wall which the film recreates. Another of Wall's most recognisable photographs, *The Crooked Path* (1991), is evoked in the fields where Coré's victims are killed and then buried, an unused stretch of overgrown dried grass in an industrial area, where activities go unnoticed. *A Hunting Scene* (1994) portrays a similar environment, tall grass beside an empty road littered with trash, an in-between

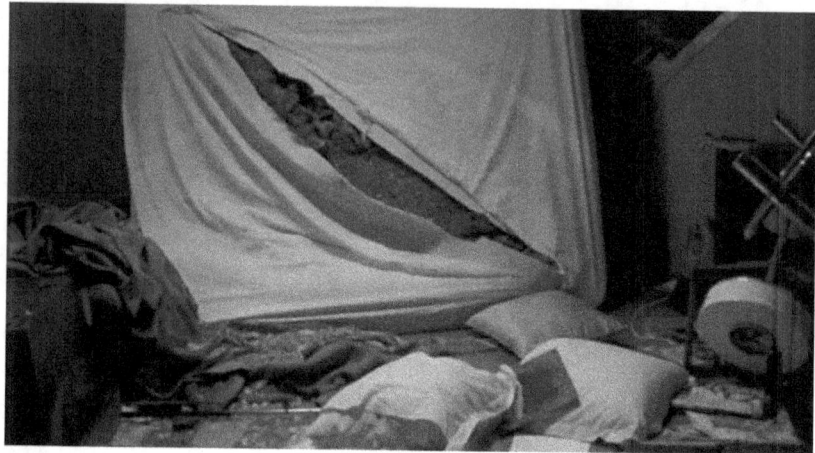

Fig. 30

place where men with guns stalk their prey. It is not hard to imagine their target being Coré, who is certainly not covering her tracks when she lures men, like the truck driver, into the grass.

The scenes in *Trouble Every Day* that draw from Wall's work evoke not just a sense of looming menace but the pain of anticipation embedded in waiting, the physical strain of constantly suppressing panic while waiting for the inevitable. Wall's images tap into this discomfort, self-contained worlds that convey an uneasiness which is increasingly palpable the longer they are looked at. Perhaps most uncomfortable is the way that this unease is shown to be an inescapable part of life, hidden in plain view, visible only to those who really look. Sotinel's (2001) apt description of the 'sensation of poisonous smoothness' in *Trouble Every Day* could equally be applied to Wall's work. The film and the photographs share a sense of disconcerting quietness that masks an undercurrent of emotions, of life and history. Phillipe Azoury (2001) compares the aesthetic of *Trouble Every Day* to the depth that lurks beneath the static surface of Wall's images, which seem to crumble under the weight of the composition at the same time as giving an impression of great emptiness. The film certainly lends itself to repeated viewing, to uncover the layers of meaning. But, ultimately, there is no definitive answer.

When writing *Trouble Every Day*, Denis was also inspired by fantastic literature, especially the work of mid-nineteenth century Irish author Le Fanu. His popular sensational fiction includes *The House by the Churchyard* (1863), *Uncle Silas* (1864) and *Carmilla* (1871), the latter of which is the most influential on cinema. The story of the innocent young Laura seduced by the vampire Mircalla is a prototype for the female vampire subgenre, with film adaptations such as the French *Blood and Roses* (*Et mourir de Plaisir*; Vadim, 1960), Spanish *The Blood Spattered Bride* (*La novia ensangrentada*; Aranda, 1972) and many Hammer films, including *The Vampire Lovers* (Ward Baker, 1970). *Trouble Every Day* is shaped by Gothic conventions, notably the genre's persistent worry about borders and boundaries. The film features gothic motifs like blood, graves, dark spaces and fire. It employs the types of the incarcerated heroine and the Faustian over-reacher, with characters who suffer through terrible dreams, madness and even suicide. Coré is a modern mad woman in the attic, a descendent of Bertha Mason in Charlotte Brontë's *Jane Eyre*, whose savage appearance is likened to a 'German spectre — the Vampyre'. Boarded up in her room by her husband, becoming increasingly unstable, Bertha sets the house on fire, determined to die, a direct parallel to Coré. Also central to the Gothic tradition is the ancestral home, a site evoked both by the Semeneau's house and also the hotel; with dark corridors and hidden areas, these locations hold many secrets.

The scene of Erwan crossing the fence to enter the Semenau property, and then the house, is straight out of a fairy-tale, like Rapunzel, where a young woman is locked away and a young hero arrives to rescue her. In an interview with Bonnaud (2001) Denis explains that while writing *Trouble Every Day* she thought about the stories transcribed by Charles Perrault which come from much older folk tales. These are enjoyable to hear as a child, she points out, but also extremely sexual, like when the ogre in Tom Thumb says it smells fresh flesh. She also mentions Beauty and the Beast, pointing out that similar imagery has existed for a long time, referencing an enigmatic Palaeolithic drawing in the Chauvet caves (discovered in 1994) of a woman's lower half merging with the form of a bison. This tale offers a familiar precedent for thinking about the animal qualities in human nature, and the innate potential for savage and monstrous behaviour. *Trouble Every Day* is inspired by two film versions of this story: Jean Renoir's La Bête humaine (1938) and also Jean Cocteau's *Beauty and the Beast*. For instance, the way that Erwan climbs the fence echoes Cocteau's film, when Avenant climbs down into the castle and is killed by an arrow shot by a statue of Diana before transforming into the beast. This in itself references the myth of Actaeon, who after seeing the goddess bathing was turned into a deer and hunted. As Shane watches June in the bath, unseen for a moment, perhaps he will be the next to be hunted? As Coré, Dalle embodies animality, growling, panting, licking and biting. Yet, she has crossed a line; she loses control of her humanity. It is Shane who more closely resembles Jacques, still living in the everyday world, plagued by a growing madness, a modern-day curse.

Cat People is another direct reference for *Trouble Every Day*, one exploring the line between human and animal, myth and the modern world. Like the seductive Irena of Tourneur's film, Coré is a beautiful and mysterious woman who is not quite human, whose transformation into something monstrous is triggered by sex. Like Irena, Coré has no control over the changes which take over her body; it is biological and, apparently, unstoppable. The recourse chosen by each woman is death, a self-sacrifice in which they take control over their fates. While Coré does not turn into an actual cat, her behavior becomes progressively animalistic as she engage in sex, forgetting what it means to be human. Panting, growling, squealing, she treats the bodies of her companions as meat, playing with it like an animal might. But she does not use them for sustenance; once they are dead she loses interest.

Denis is also influenced by contemporary horror directors. Specifically, she cites Brian De Palma's *Dressed to Kill* (1980) and Abel Ferrara's *The Addiction* (1995) as the films that most influenced *Trouble Every Day*. The opening scene of *Dressed to Kill* is a striking example of voyeurism, setting up a relationship between gaze and touch. Travelling through a bedroom into a bathroom, the camera reveals Kate in the shower, fixating on her naked body, which she strokes erotically. Though the glass shower is a typical site of specularisation in cinema, this behaviour is not for her husband, who is not watching, or even the viewer, who is unseen. Rather, it is her desire that is the impulse, her gaze that we inhabit when we look through the water running down the glass. This ownership of sexual feelings is reflected by Coré, who is overwhelmed by desire much like Kate, though her extra-marital affairs progress past the sex to murder. *The Addiction* is also about desire, not sexual but rather for a substance – the blood-filled syringes are a clear substitute for heroin. Using vampirism as a metaphor for drug addiction, Ferrara asks what it means to be human, about violence enacted collectively as well as in intimate relationships, questions Denis is also deeply interested in. Kathleen, a philosophy student, is transformed into a vampire, a creature who lives by different rules and needs. She becomes the evil which previously had been only academic for her. Like Coré, who researched the libido as an objective subject before finding herself taken over by it, theory becomes lived experience. Both Kathleen and Coré are changed by outside forces, driven by desire, their need for more leading to similarly gruesome murderous frenzies.

ART-HORROR AND CROSSING GENRES

Denis has a strong familiarity with, and appreciation for, genre cinema. Early in her career, she worked on several avant-garde films that aligned with exploitation cinema, such as *La messe dorée* (Montresor, 1975) and *Zoo zéro* (Fleischer, 1979). Eduardo de Gregorio's *Sérail* (1976), a mystery about an English novelist and a crumbling mansion inhabited by two mysterious women, must have stoked Denis' familiarity with the Gothic tradition which manifests in *Trouble Every Day*. In interviews with Yann Gonzalez (2001) and Marie-Claude Harrer (2001b) about *Trouble Every Day*, she considers the economic relationship between the horror genre and the film industry, which mainly existed in Italy and the United States. In these low-budget productions, everything is recycled: sets, costumes and even actors and directors like Roger Corman, who she admired as a student. Denis also points out how genre films deflect censorship, with monsters and vampires a way to break restrictions on showing sexuality on screen. Yet, Denis also understands the history of horror as a spectacle in France. To Bonnaud (2001), she describes Dalle's performance in *Trouble Every Day* as beautiful and poetic 'something that belonged to the cinema and not to the Grand Guignol'. Founded in 1897, the Grand Guignol is a style of a horror stage show named for a theatre in Montmartre, which shocked audiences with violent and gory scenes performed with realistic effects. By distancing her film from this type of over-the-top performance, Denis emphasises that the violence in her film is not gratuitous or unduly graphic. It is part of the narrative but not its sole purpose; she is inspired as much by the subtle terror of a Tourneur film as the dramatic excess of a filmmaker like Argento.

Trouble Every Day employs a litany of visual tropes from the horror genre: a body laid out in the grass; a killer seducing his/her prey; blood soaked sheets; a woman looking out a window; a woman in a bath; a secret lab; a burning house. Many of these are tied to the gothic tradition, such as Coré wandering through her house in a white nightdress stained with blood. The opening scene of a couple kissing in a car is another trope in the genre, where sex is punished by death. Though it is present in early cinema, such as *Night of Terror* (Stoloff, 1933), it gained popularity through a combination of urban legends and the real-life Texarkana murders of 1946, the basis for *The Town That Dreaded Sundown* (Pierce, 1976). The way that Shane stalks the woman down the street is also a familiar scene, a killer pursuing his intended prey. The anxiety provoked as he follows her is heightened later on the bus, where he leans so close to the woman in front of him that his nose almost touches her (Fig. 31). When the camera takes his point of view, a technique especially prominent in slasher films, it increases anticipation of what will happen to the victim. Phillipe Met (2003) proposes that severing these ties to recognisable tropes would have helped Denis escape objections to 'a genre film redeemed—or damned—as an "arty" film, or conversely, of auteurism parading as horror'. Yet, without them, the film would be stripped of much of its depth.

Fig. 31

In *Trouble Every Day*, Denis applies an art film aesthetic to horror themes. The way that it crosses genres – art, horror, sci-fi, drama – is perhaps one reason for its poor reception on its release. It is too distasteful for most of Denis' established audience, many won over by *Beau Travail*, with the violence of the final act especially confounding and alienating. Yet, many horror fans are unenthused by the slow elliptical narrative, where the gore is held back until the end and performed without any theatricality. Denis ignores many characteristics expected in a horror film. She focuses on slowly building a sense of persistent dread and lingering sense of danger rather than surprising the viewer with tactics such as jump scares. 'I've seen many films that try to surprise the audience with violence. I find it very artificial,' she remarks (in Smith 2002). Most viewers are likely disappointed by the films refusal of a cathartic conclusion – Shane will presumably leave Paris and become a serial killer in America. They are left with more questions than answers. Lalanne (2001) writes that while *Trouble Every Day* crosses genres it does not settle, its only territory affect and sensation. Yet, viewers undoubtedly seek to classify the film so as to help understand it, especially as it is so low on direct exposition. By denying a firm position in a genre and by being, overall, a very difficult film to watch, it left the majority of its audience wanting something different.

MONSTER MOVIES

Trouble Every Day evokes the tradition of the monster movie, especially those from classic cinema. In the 1930s, horror films became a popular and relatively inexpensive money-making option for many production houses, notably Universal Studios. Many featured monsters based on popular literature, such as Bram Stoker's *Dracula* (1897), Mary Shelley's *Frankenstein* (1818), Robert Louis Stevenson's *Strange Case of Dr Jekyll and Mr Hyde* (1886), H.G. Wells' *The Invisible Man* (1896) and *The Island of Dr Moreau* (1896). They became increasingly familiar to viewers, establishing precedents for many of the creatures that continue to attract cinemagoers, like vampires, werewolves and zombies. While these are all very different types, what connects them is that they were once mortal. These formerly human, or semi-human, creatures look like people but no longer live as them. Separate from the rules that regulate society, they represent a fear of the animal nature of humans, of base instincts and savage behaviour. They also suggest anxieties about the body which *Trouble Every Day* relies on, emphasising its fragile physicality, made of flesh, bones and blood. There are several images in the film drawn from classic horror films. Thrilled by her escape, Coré stretches her coat out like a cape, or wings (Fig. 32), a vampiric image which brings to mind Bela Lugosi as Dracula or, a later example, Delphine Seyrig in *Daughters of Darkness* (Kümel, 1971). There is also a possible nod to the 1915 crime series *Les Vampires*, where the dancer Marfa performs in a bat costume, stretching her wings as she swoops around the stage (though, it is actually June who later wears a hooded black cape). Shane also mimics Lugosi's Dracula, opening his eyes exaggeratedly wide and snarling to make June laugh on a balcony at Notre-Dame (Fig. 33). Curling his hands, he also evokes Lon Chaney in *Phantom of the Opera* (1925). He picks June up briefly, like Quasimodo in *The Hunchback of Notre Dame* before lurching towards her, arms outstretched like the monster in *Frankenstein* (Whale, 1931). June plays along, laughing and she shrinks back, raising her arms in a pantomime of a classic horror victim. Shane also echoes the dual personality of Jekyll and Hyde, whose experiments on himself tapped into his dark urges. Both are scientists who try to subdue their alter-egos, impulsive and violent, assaulting and murdering at will.

Figs. 32 & 33

The affliction that plagues Coré and Shane seems to strip back their humanity, turning them into something else. But: what? While Coré's symbols painted in blood remind us of magical sigils, and her body is set alight, she is not a witch. She is animal-like, but not a shapeshifter. Feeding off sex, Coré evokes the mythological succubus, which goes by many names in folklore around the world, yet she is decisively not supernatural and gains no power from her acts. She is frequently described as a vampire by critics, scholars and even by Denis herself. 'Think of "Trouble Every Day" as Dracula with pretensions,' remarks Holden (2002). This type offers an acceptable motivation for Coré's allure, with her seduction and her desires aligned with the hypnotic power of figures like Dracula. But Coré is not exactly a vampire. The vampire is usually male, with fangs an obvious stand-in for the phallus; the aforementioned Carmilla is one significant exception. It is also typically intelligent and calculating, guided by reason as much as biology. Coré, however, demonstrates a slow disintegration of the psyche, with no evidence of thought beyond escaping so she can satisfy her hunger. She eats flesh instead of drinking blood, devouring bodies messily rather than leaving a neat pair of small puncture wounds. It is for her enjoyment, not nourishment. Because she actually consumes her victims, shown visibly chewing, she is undeniably a cannibal. Obviously, the vampire is a much more palatable figure, its behaviour explained by supernatural origins and acceptable because this separates it from humanity. However, Coré is decisively human.

Léo's research specialty suggests that Coré has a drug-induced neurological condition which can be explained by science, to an extent. Having regressed to a state of id, reduced to state where she is almost no longer human, Coré is much more closely aligned with the zombie than the vampire. Shane, it seems, is earlier in this process, fighting this deterioration. While they are not undead, like zombies, perhaps a part of them is. What would the scientists find if it was their brains they were slicing up in the lab to look at under a microscope? Zombies are, essentially, an expression of hunger. Whether corpses reanimated under the control of a person, like in much early cinema, post-1960s zombies created by a virus or nuclear radiation or the newer style of impossibly fast zombies, they are a reflection of base instincts. This is also at the heart of the werewolf genre, which again reflects the dismissal of expectations around human behaviour. The werewolf is a metaphor for the animal within, which is – dangerously – always there. It only emerges for a few days a month, let loose with the full moon. The creature is all the more dangerous as, for most of the time, it appears human, living among the society that it endangers with its existence. However it is not the lunar cycle that instigates Coré and Shane's changes, which do not follow a neat, regular calendar but are possible at any time.

SCIENCE GONE WRONG

Trouble Every Day is part of a subgenre about scientific research gone awry, which is often tied to monster movies. These films point to the danger of overstepping, of playing god and disturbing the natural order, questioning what it means to be human. This is especially notable when involving human testing, such as in *The Crimson Stain*

Mystery (Hunter, 1916), *Island of Lost Souls* (Kenton, 1932) – based on *The Island of Doctor Moreau*, *The Fly* (Neumann, 1958 and Cronenberg, 1986), *Altered States* (Russell, 1980) and various adaptations of *Dr. Jekyll and Mr. Hyde*. Coré and Shane demonstrate what can go wrong when the body is altered on a biological level, losing their humanity. Narratively, one of the closest films to *Trouble Every Day* is *Shivers* (1975), David Cronenberg's first feature film. A doctor experimenting on parasites creates an aphrodisiac that causes uncontrollable sexual desire in its host and which transmit through sexual contact. After successfully implanting them in his lover, the parasites quickly infect others in the apartment complex. *Shivers* overtly references anxieties surrounding sexually transmitted infections and also, like *Trouble Every Day*, around desire, infidelity and violence. Similar themes are addressed in Todd Haynes' first feature film *Poison* (1991), which weaves together three separate stories, one of which is especially close to *Trouble Every Day*. Shot as a low-budget mid-century sci-fi, 'Horror' follows a doctor who makes a scientific breakthrough by creating a serum that synthesises the human sex drive. When accidentally ingested, he becomes a carrier for a contagion which manifests as oozing pustules and violent impulses. Breeding lust and disease, it spreads through the city. The biological conditions in both *Shivers* and *Poison* drive the hosts mad, completely overwhelming their creators, until they commit suicide, much like Coré.

BODY HORROR

Body horror is a strong feature of *Trouble Every Day*, linking it to monster movies, sci-fi films and the New French Extremity. Many of the films mentioned above tap into the fear and disgust provoked when the body is made wrong. An overarching element of the subgenre is anxiety about the body, which is fragile and easily manipulated – skin tears, bones crack, fluids ooze and organs unravel. Most body horror features obvious exterior changes to the body: it might be cut open, expel organic material or grow into something else. However, it is broad enough to encompass a range of narratives. A supernatural force might create physical changes to the body, which transforms into something inhuman. The body might distort in a way that is impossible when possessed by an entity like a demon or ghost. Its hideous and unnatural decay can be explained by contagion – a zombie epidemic, an alien parasite, a supernatural virus. Sometimes changes to the body are due to human intervention, which is the case in *Trouble Every Day*, where scientific experiments go wrong and the potential for the body to be dangerously manipulated is underestimated. Trouble Every Day engages with body horror not in its depiction of Coré and Shane, as the monsters, but rather the treatment of Erwan and Christelle. Their bodies are handled like meat, penetrated and ruined. The gore in the two vicious scenes is grotesque, physically affective. Flesh is mutilated and blood escapes, no longer contained inside as it should be. Denis specifically mentions liking Cronenberg, whose oeuvre and reputation was built on body horror. Following *Shivers*, films such as *The Brood* (1979) and *Crash* (1996) hinge on the connection between sex and violence, crossing the line between horror and pleasure. *Trouble Every Day* aligns with this crisis, with the treatment of the body on screen affecting the body of the viewer.

SICKENING CINEMA

When an ambulance was called for two women who fainted at the premier of *Trouble Every Day*, the film became part of a notorious category of sickening cinema. There is a long history of viewers becoming physically ill while watching horror films. Pre-code examples like Tod Browning's *Dracula* and *Freaks* (1932) revealed that, paradoxically, such responses could actually encourage interest, both for viewers and the press, and so ticket sales. This response was positioned as a marketing tool, enticing audiences to experience just how scandalous these films were for themselves. Sometimes it was manufactured, or at least manipulated, by studios and cinemas. For instance, in 1935 a first-aid booth was prominently installed in the lobby of the Palace Theatre in Chicago when it screened *Bride of Frankenstein* (Whale, 1935). Loew's Majestic Theatre in Bridgeport planted a woman in each audience of *Mark of the Vampire* to scream and faint, then be carried out to an ambulance waiting in front of the theatre. Producer/director William Castle was renowned for devising gimmicks for screenings of his films, such as giving ticket-holders to *Macabre* (Castle, 1958) a $1,000 life insurance policy in case they died of fright. Drawing on this history, the tagline for *The Last House on the Left* (Craven, 1972) warned 'To avoid fainting, keep repeating: "It's only a movie".'

Physically affective films that sickened viewers, with some even fainting, over the past two decades include: *Audition* (Miike, 1999), *Ichi the Killer* (Miike, 2001), *Wolf Creek* (McLean 2005), *Hostel* (Roth, 2005), *Saw III* (Bousman, 2006), *Martyrs* (Laugier, 2008), *Van Diemen's Land* (Heide, 2009), *Antichrist* (von Trier, 2009), *127 Hours* (Boyle, 2010), *A Serbian Film* (Spasojevic, 2010), *Snowtown* (Kurzel, 2011), *The Woman* (McKee, 2011), *Goodnight Mommy* (Franz and Fiala, 2014), *Raw* (Ducournau, 2016), Kuso (Flying Lotus, 2017) and *The House That Jack Built* (von Trier, 2018). There are also numerous reports of a Kansas woman who suffered a heart attack and died while viewing Mel Gibson's *Passion of the Christ* in 2004. These films all attest to the affective potential of cinema, which Denis taps into in *Trouble Every Day*.

A CINEMATIC HISTORY OF EXTREME VIOLENCE

Trouble Every Day is part of a long tradition of violence on screen, with filmmakers pushing the boundaries of how far an image could go. The 1929 silent Surrealist film *Un Chien Andalou* is a predecessor to Denis' representation of violence and also desire. Directed by Luis Buñuel, who co-wrote the film with Salvador Dalí, it was inspired by a dream each man had, of a cloud slicing the moon in half like a razor blade slicing through an eye and a hand crawling with ants. Of the apparently nonsensical arrangement of scenes, the most famous is of a razor held to a woman's eye which is sliced open in a grotesque close-up. This exacting scalpel is echoed in *Eyes Without a Face* (Franju, 1960), when, with skilled precision, a doctor cuts into his victim's face with a surprising level of verisimilitude. The grisly realism in scenes such as these is echoed by the special effects in *Trouble Every Day* when Coré attacks Erwan, where the focus on realism deepens the distress provoked by the story. At the Cannes press conference, Denis clarified 'I don't set out to shock. That's not my way of doing things. I don't think it's explicit.' However, the violence in *Trouble Every Day* unsurprisingly did shock the audience. While it might not be as explicit and bloody as other films from the same period, it is incredibly disturbing and horrifying.

1960s-1970s

Trouble Every Day is indebted to the increasing levels of violence, sex and nudity depicted in cinema of the 1960s and 1970s. In 1968, the Hays code, which had governed US cinema since the 1930s, was officially updated, with the loosening of restrictions in the ratings system making room for more explicit content. Many narratives in horror films of this period changed from monsters to more realistic threats. Danger transitions from outside forces to more local threats, often encountered outside of cities, with *Two Thousand Maniacs!* (Lewis, 1964), *Texas Chain Saw Massacre* and *The Hills Have Eyes* (Craven, 1977) notable US examples. Many films of this period also have perpetrators who are seemingly normal humans who undertake explicit scenes of sexual violence, such as *A Clockwork Orange* (Kubrick, 1971), *Straw Dogs* (Peckinpah, 1971) and the rape-revenge *I Spit on Your Grave* (Zarchi, 1978), a direct precedent to Noe's *Irreversible*, with extended rape scenes that prove unwatchable and which no amount of vengeance makes up for. The atrocities shown in these films often serve as metaphors for social issues. For instance, Wes Craven's *The Last House on the Left* is a response to the seemingly pointless horrors of the Vietnam War, the first televised war. Similarly, in *Salò, or the 120 Days of Sodom* (1975), Pier Paolo Pasolini pointedly set Sade's novel during Mussolini's fascist regime. Denis admits that this is the only film she has had to walk out of: 'It took me three times to watch the whole thing. I think I always stopped at [the scene of] eating the nails. The first time, I had to leave! I came the week after to see the film [again], and I knew this scene was going to assault me. I said, "I will close my eyes and I will stay this time." But I had to leave again. The third time, I made it' (in Dallas 2013).

ITALIAN CANNIBAL EXPLOITATION

An indirect predecessor to *Trouble Every Day* is the Italian cannibal exploitation genre, which peaked in the decade between 1972 and 1982. Featuring extreme violence and excessive gore, distribution of these films was often limited (several were listed as 'video nasties' in the UK ion the 1980s, making their distribution actually illegal). In examples like *Last Cannibal World* (Deodato, 1977), *The Mountain of the Cannibal God* (Martino, 1978) and *Cannibal Ferox* (Lenzi, 1981) the characters venture into the South American jungle seeking to exploit its untapped natural resources, with their deaths framed as punishment for this violation. Like adventure films from the 1930-1950s, where characters end up in inhospitable jungles, threatened by dangerous terrain, animals and – sometimes – bloodthirsty tribes, this ties into an interest in exploration. More than just violent deaths and schlocky effects, the subgenre reflects anxieties surrounding colonialism, exploiting the fear of the other. Its most infamous entry, 1980's *Cannibal Holocaust*, directly addresses this colonial narrative, positioning its crew of documentary filmmakers as intruders with no regard for life. They manipulate the tribe they are there to apparently study, trying to generate sensationalist footage to fit their audience's expectations. They are the real savages. *Cannibal Holocaust* questions what we as an audience will watch, and often demand, of films, including violence that is close to – or actually – unwatchable. While *Trouble Every Day* is not set in the jungle, with no mention of bloodthirsty tribes, it does explore the idea of the other, which weaves throughout Denis' filmography. More specifically, the origin of the affliction Coré and Shane share is a plant discovered in the jungle in Guyana, where they were part of Léo's team conducting botanical research, tying into the idea of the danger of the unknown, that places unexplored and unmanaged by Western powers hold untold dangers. That Shane joined Léo's research expedition looking for financial gain suggests the condition might be his comeuppance.

VIDEO NASTIES

Fuelled by a tabloid-led moral panic, the Video Nasty phenomenon arose in the 1980s, an infamous label coined in the United Kingdom in response to the increasingly graphic content of many horror films available on home video. Found to violate the Obscene Publications Act, video nasties were deemed inappropriate for distribution. The term covered a wide range of films, from Michael Findlay grindhouse to Argento gialli. Of a list of 72 films, 39 were prosecuted, including many now considered classics, like *Cannibal Holocaust*, *The Last House on the Left*, *The Driller Killer* (Ferrara, 1979), *A Bay of Blood* (Bava, 1971) and *Tenebre* (Argento, 1982). However, a much longer unofficial list of titles grew. These films were banned not just in the UK but across the world; many were released with cuts and only re-released uncut years, even decades, after they were made. However, filmmakers continued to push the boundaries despite the obstacles of censorship. In the 1990s, New Brutalism honed in on portraying violence on screen, with a focus on realism which ties to *Trouble Every Day*. Films like *Man Bites Dog* (Belvaux, Bonzel and Poelvoorde, 1992), *Bad Lieutenant* (Ferrara, 1992), *Reservoir Dogs* (Tarantino, 1992) and *Natural Born Killers* (Stone, 1994) shocked viewers with their intentionally casual approach to graphic violence. Scenes of murder, torture and assault – with realistic effects – imply a certain desensitisation, not just for the characters but also the audience. Like some of the examples above, such as *The Last House on the Left* and *Cannibal Holocaust*, these films provoke viewers, challenging what they will actually sit through, what they get out of watching such horror. They are a direct predecessor to *Trouble Every Day* and, more broadly, New French Extremity.

NEW FRENCH EXTREMITY

In 2004, film critic James Quandt coined the term New French Extremity in a discussion about a trend for hyper-violence and graphic sex in recent cinema. Starting with Bruno Dumont's then newly-released *Twentynine Palms* (2003), Quandt referenced *Trouble Every Day* alongside films such as *Sombre* (Grandrieux, 1998), *Les Amants criminels* (Ozon, 1999), *Romance* (Breillat, 1999), *Baise-moi* (Despentes and Trinh Thi, 2000), Noe's *Irréversible* and *In My Skin* (de Van, 2002). Such films, he argues derisively, seemed determined to break every taboo, co-opting themes and images from splatter films, exploitation flicks and pornography. For Quandt, such low-brow references sully what he describes as 'the high-art environs of a national cinema', reflecting how, as discussed earlier, the blending of high and low genres in films often leads to their poor reception. Of *Trouble Every Day* he claims: 'An enervated Denis barely musters a hint of narrative to contain or explain the orgiastic bloodletting; a shadow plot involving Vincent Gallo as an American doctor struggling with his own bloodlust while on honeymoon in Paris is both cursory and ludicrous.' An important point to rebut here is that Shane receives more screen time, character development and dialogue than Coré, with the two stories parallel rather than weighted.

New French Extremity developed through the early twentieth-first century, with notable additions including *Haute Tension* (Aja, 2003), *Ils* (Moreau and Palud, 2006), *À l'intérieur*

(Bustillo and Maury, 2007), *Frontière(s)* (Gens, 2007) and 2008's *Martyrs*. Presenting taboos being broken in graphic detail – torture, rape, incest, cannibalism – these films generated mixed critical responses. Quandt was certainly not alone in his criticism. Yet, while many critics disliked, maybe even disapproved of, New French Extremity, it had an audience. Importantly, this impulse was not just confined to France, with international examples of hyper-violent cinema including *Calvaire* (Welz, 2004) in Belgium, *Funny Games* (Haneke, 1997) in Austria, *Wolf Creek* in Australia, *Dogville* (von Trier, 2003) in Denmark, *Oldboy* (Park, 2003) in South Korea, *Szamanka* (Zulawski, 1996) in Poland and *Audition* in Japan. In the US, the co-called 'torture porn' subgenre was named for an influx of these films in a post-9/11 context, including *House of 1000 Corpses* (Zombie, 2003), *Saw* (Wan, 2004) and *Hostel* (Roth, 2005). The representation of extreme violence was not just limited to art films or to Hollywood, but was a far-reaching trend.

Positioning *Trouble Every Day* as part of a group of films in the late twentieth and early twenty-first centuries that pushed the boundaries of style and violence emphasises its place in a broader movement. It is not alone in its unflinching (mis)treatment of the body in startlingly brutal ways on screen, though of course Denis crafts her own approach to filming this horror. The move to realistic portrayals of violence and sex around the turn of the century is, like the cinema before it, a response to socio-historical concerns. When read as such, these films can be considered as symptomatic and also critical of the world. They respond to how violence on screen is often real, with reportage showing footage of war and deaths livestreamed over the internet. They comment on the way that bodies are treated on both a micro and macro level, by individuals and the government. They point to anxieties around control – both lack of and excess. *Trouble Every Day* is a film that shows there remain things in this world that are terrifyingly unknown, with no answers or solutions.

5. THE LEGACY OF *TROUBLE EVERY DAY*

A film that is at once demanding, beautiful, infuriating, distressing, elusive and captivating, *Trouble Every Day* demands in-depth exploration. As part of the filmography of a significant and respected director whose career in cinema spans almost five decades, it deserves attention not despite but because of its poor reception. Since its release, *Trouble Every Day* has received some critical reassessment, found a place in many best-of horror lists and slowly reached new audiences. While the film was always going to be deeply divisive, it might have proved more successful if made several years later. Through digital publications and social media, it likely would have generated word of mouth interest and more discussions about the film aside from published reviews. Also, distribution might have been less spread out: after its premier at Cannes in May 2001, it took several years to be released across the world, reaching London in December 2002 and the Melbourne International Film Festival not until August 2003. Primarily showing at festivals, its audience was largely limited to DVD releases. In the 2010s, the cross-genre art-horror also found a wider audience, in films like horror-western *A Girl Walks Home Alone at Night* (Amirpour, 2014), horror-sci-fi *Under the Skin* (Glazer, 2013) and horror-crime *I Saw the Devil* (Kim, 2010). Of course, this brings to mind recent discussions of 'prestige horror' or 'post-horror', labels created with the aim of establishing a taxonomy for films that do not fit into the narrowest view of the genre (low-budget B-movies, slashers or otherwise gratuitous violence). These labels initially stem from the uninformed and flawed position that well-made and thought-provoking horror films about bigger issues are a new development, although there is a body of critical work emerging that engages fruitfully with them (e.g. Church 2021)

First screened in 2001 and released gradually over the next two years, *Trouble Every Day* was released in the midst of a surge in explicit violence on screen in the late-1990s and early 2000s. Early twenty-first century horror was driven by provoking disgust by representing violence enacted on and by the body. Some films seem to take this physical repulsion as their primary aim. Responses to *Trouble Every Day* are inevitably inflected by this broader trend, which led to the classification of the new subgenres of New French Extremity and its popular counterpart 'torture porn', which gained popularity in post-9/11 US. Denis is certainly not the only auteur to make a film featuring violence that shocked audiences during in this period. A close counterpart to *Trouble Every Day* is Marina de Van's *In My Skin*, released the following year. The violence in both films is closely bound to desire, which is expressed by women in both. But in *In My Skin*, the overwhelming need for incorporation is turned inwards. Where Coré is a woman who searches for men to satisfy her lust for flesh, Esther devours her own. De Van's portrayal of cannibalism is just as painful to watch as Denis', with both showing the mutilation of the body with straightforward realism. A more recent film that draws comparison to *Trouble Every Day* is Julia Ducournau's *Raw*. Uncontrollable desire manifests as hunger in the world of protagonist Justine, a young woman who exerts control in a world where she feels she does not have any. *Trouble Every Day* helped to carve out space for the realistic portrayal of desire and flesh on screen.

After *Trouble Every Day*, Denis continued pushing the boundaries of genre. *Bastards* is one of the closest films in tone to *Trouble Every Day*, another horrific mystery that revolves around sexual violence. The bleak neo-noir explores family and vengeance, with the final piece of the puzzle revealed in a sickening conclusion. *Let the Sunshine In* deals with the idea of love under the guise of a romantic-comedy, but, again, by not neatly fitting into its taxonomy, was met with some confusion. Most recently at the time of writing, *High Life*, released in 2019, is a hybrid sci-fi art film with a similar focus on the overreaching scientist and experimentations on human sexuality. A decisive move into US market, this is Denis' first solely English-language film (of course, *Trouble Every Day* is predominantly in English with just a little French), and also has a larger budget than she would usually work with (around €8 million, compared to €3.8 for *Trouble Every Day* or €3.6 for *35 Shots of Rum*). Starring Robert Pattinson and Juliette Binoche, it was guaranteed to create interest. Another drawcard was the involvement of the artist Olafur Eliasson in the production design. Denis and Eliasson began their collaboration in 2014; she made the short film *Contact* based on tests he was performing for his new work of the same name. The all-encompassing amber light in this installation appears in the conclusion of *High Life*. Like *Trouble Every Day*, the film was in development for about a decade, with numerous changes in funding, script and casting. It was also poorly received by many critics and cinemagoers, misunderstood by those unfamiliar with Denis' work and expecting a more conventional sci-fi film. Overall, her most ambitious films which stretch the boundaries of genre are the most divisive.

Denis' international stature as a filmmaker is especially impressive as she is a woman in an industry with far more men directors. However, a recurrent point in interviews is her dislike at being labelled a 'female director'. When asked by Damon Smith (2002) if she felt pressure to address certain issues as a woman director, she replies: 'In a way, it's impossible…I think making films deals with something more important than a role and/or being only a woman director. I only to try to be the best I am as a human being.' In a much later interview, she insists: 'Female director? I feel like I am an animal. I am a female director like this is a female bird. No, I am a director' (in Clarke 2018). Denis does acknowledge, however, that she realised she had to take control in her work: 'Suddenly, it was a sort of game for me. Not to be masculine. To be indestructible' (in Cochrane 2009). For instance, when making *Ni une ni deux*, a short for French television about four Cameroonian women, she was advised to add a voice-over, even though all the participants spoke French, just with an accent. 'I said I thought it was a shame that these women couldn't speak for themselves, that it had to be me who told their stories,' recalls Denis. 'This was using the voice-over to objectify the women, so it wasn't acceptable to me' (in Mayne 2005). Denis' frustration at the label of woman director is understandable – having an entire oeuvre filtered through gender is reductive and unfair. However, it is still significant that Denis is a highly acclaimed and successful director in a field dominated by men. In 2018, just 8% of the top 250 top-grossing movies in the US were directed by women. Of the top-grossing 1200 films from 2007-2018, just 4.3% of directors were women. In France specifically, films directed or co-directed by women grew from 20.8% in 2008 to 27% in 2017. While this points to a cultural difference between Hollywood and European cinema, there are still notable differences in other factors in France. For instance, in 2017 the average budget gap between films made by women and men was €2 million and distribution spend was 34% less for those that were women-directed. As much as it is not fair to only consider Denis' film through her gender, it must have been a factor in at least some aspects of her work. It is an impressive feat to establish and maintain a long-term career as a director; it is even more so when faced with inherent bias because of gender.

Trouble Every Day is a difficult, unflinching film, but one that is narratively and stylistically stimulating. Close exploration of its assembly of images reveals a broad range of visual, literary and non-fiction references. It is part of a lineage of genre cinema, a film that challenges the audience. There are manifold reasons why it was so poorly received – its cross-genre art/horror classification, graphic violence, expectations of Denis as a filmmaker and of cinema more broadly. The quiet, cold aesthetic is a surface which barely hides an overwhelming weight of feeling and history. The hypnotic images of bodies plunge the viewer into its depths of anxiety, desire and dangerous urges. *Trouble Every Day* lends itself – even requires – repeated viewing, in order to push through the layers, much like Core and Shane excavate the body. But, the inside is already on the outside. Ultimately, there are no definitive answers to the questions the film asks. It offers no catharsis, leaving the viewer with a lingering sense of unease. *Trouble Every Day* is a profoundly uncomfortable experience which leaves its mark, like June's bruise. Its lasting impact on viewers, the way that the film lingers, not just for hours but years, is a sign of great filmmaking.

Acknowledgements

This book is dedicated to my parents, Steve and Allana, who could never have anticipated how integral film would become to my life. Fridays were movie nights at our house and through my teenage years we saw almost everything that was released at our local suburban video store, which, admittedly, had a very limited scope of stock. On weekends, I often watched the black-and-white midday movies on television my mother switched on as she ironed, a seemingly haphazard jumble of melodramas, Elvis musicals, film noir and the occasional western. My father took my professed love of horror seriously enough to rent *The Exorcist* on VHS for us to watch when I was, really, much too young. Even though my mother realised how absolutely terrified I was and turned it off, it did not deter either of them from introducing me to more classics. They rented *The Omen* and let me stay up to watch *Silence of the Lambs* when it came on TV late one night. During school holidays, they would hand over the video shop membership card as I chose stacks of old VHS cases from the weekly section based almost entirely on the covers. As an adult, I tentatively branched out beyond mainstream cinema and English-language title and as my watch list swelled, so did my enthusiasm. Eventually, I would aim to stoke the same level of curiosity and excitement when teaching art history and film studies at the University of Sydney.

Blake has been the one to witness—and contend with—my growing obsession with cinema, encouraging my transition to writing about film and supporting my decision to sign onto another book while my first and third were in progress. Trying to find a way to express my gratitude leaves me, for once, speechless.

Special thanks also go to John Atkinson, who agreed that this was the film for me to write about for Auteur – it was an exciting and terrifying challenge.

Bibliography

Alberge, D. (2001). 'Director Defends Cannes Film's Brutal Sex Scenes', *The Times*, 8 May. Available at: http://ezproxy.nypl.org/login?url=https://search-proquest-com.i.ezproxy.nypl.org/docview/318490120?accountid=35635 (Accessed: 5 March 2019).

Ancian, A. (2002). 'Claire Denis: An Interview'. Translated by Inge Pruks. *Senses of Cinema*, 23 (November-December). Available at: http://sensesofcinema.com/2002/spotlight-claire-denis/denis_interview/ (Accessed: 28 February 2018).

Anderson, J. (2002). 'A Marriage Made in Heaven: Stuart Staples on Tindersticks' Claire Denis Film Scores'. *Cinema scope*, 47. Available at: http://cinema-scope.com/cinema-scope-magazine/interviews-a-marriage-made-in-heaven-stuart-staples-on-tindersticks-claire-denis-film-scores/ (Accessed: 28 February 2018).

Augé, M. (1995). *Non-places: introduction to an anthropology of supermodernity*. Translated by John Howe. London; New York: Verso.

Azoury, P. (2001). 'En écho aux photos de Jeff Wall', *Libération*, July 11. Available at: https://next.liberation.fr/culture/2001/07/11/en-echo-aux-photos-de-jeff-wall_371252 (Accessed: 28 February 2018).

Baumgarten, M. (2002). 'Trouble Every Day', *Austin Chronicle*, 26 July. Available at: https://www.austinchronicle.com/events/film/2002-07-26/trouble-every-day/ (Accessed: 28 February 2018).

Berenstein, R.J. (2015). '"It Will Thrill You, It Will Terrify You, It Might Even Horrify You": Gender, Reception, and Classic Horror Cinema', in Grant, B.K. (ed.) *The dread of difference: gender and the horror film*. Austin: University of Texas Press, pp. 145-170.

Beugnet, M. (2004). *Claire Denis*. Manchester; New York: Manchester University Press.

Bonnaud, F. (2000). 'Trouble Every Day', *Les Inrockuptibles*, 30 November. Available at: https://www.lesinrocks.com/cinema/films-a-l-affiche/trouble-every-day-2/ (Accessed: 28 February 2018).

Bonnaud, F. (2001) 'Claire Denis', *Les Inrockuptibles*, 3 June. Available at: https://www.lesinrocks.com/2001/07/03/cinema/actualite-cinema/claire-denis-lecons-de-tenebre-11218407/ (Accessed: 28 February 2018).

Bowen, C. (2013). 'Trouble Every Day', *Slant*, October 6. Available at: https://www.slantmagazine.com/film/review/trouble-every-day-2013 (Accessed: 28 February 2018).

Bradshaw, P. (2002). 'Trouble Every Day', *The Guardian*, 19 December. Available at: https://www.theguardian.com/culture/2002/dec/20/artsfeatures7 (Accessed: 28 February 2018).

Chalmers, R. (2015). 'Béatrice Dalle is the ultimate femme fatale', GQ, 27 February. Available at: https://www.gq-magazine.co.uk/article/beatrice-dalle-robert-chalmers-betty-blue-femme-fatale (Accessed: 28 February 2018).

Chauvin, J-S. (2001). 'Au-delà des genres', *Les cahiers du cinéma* n°559, Juillet-Aout.

Church, D. (2021). *Post-Horror: Art, Genre and Cultural Elevation*. Edinburgh: Edinburgh University Press.

Clarke, D. (2018). 'Claire Denis: 'We are normal people. Even though we are French', *Irish Times*, 14 April. Available at: https://www.irishtimes.com/culture/film/claire-denis-we-are-normal-people-even-though-we-are-french-1.3457322 (Accessed: 5 March 2019).

Cochrane, K. (2009). 'I'm not interested in making conclusions', *The Guardian*, 3 July. Available at: https://www.theguardian.com/film/2009/jul/03/claire-denis-french-director-interview (Accessed: 28 February 2018).

Creed, B. (1993). *The Monstrous-Feminine: Film, Feminism, Psychoanalysis*. London; New York: Routledge.

Creutz, N. (2001). 'Claire Denis au rendez-vous de la peur', *Le temps*, 11 July. Available at: https://www.letemps.ch/culture/claire-denis-rendezvous-peur (Accessed: 28 February 2018).

Dallas, P. (2013). 'Claire Denis, Under the Skin', *Interview*, October 23. Available at: https://www.interviewmagazine.com/film/claire-denis-bastards (Accessed: 28 February 2018).

Danel, I. (2001). 'Sang pour sang', *Les Echos*, 11 July. Available at: https://www.lesechos.fr/11/07/2001/LesEchos/18442-123-ECH_sang-pour-sang.htm (Accessed: 28 February 2018).

Darke, C. (2000). 'Desire is Violence', *Sight & Sound Magazine*, 10 (7), pp. 16-18. Available at: http://old.bfi.org.uk/sightandsound/feature/30 (Accessed: 28 February 2018).

Dawson, T. (2002). 'Béatrice Dalle', *BBC*, 17 December. http://www.bbc.co.uk/films/2002/12/17/beatrice_dalle_trouble_every_day_interview.shtml. (Accessed: 28 February 2018).

Dazed (2011). 'Claire Denis & Tindersticks', *Dazed*, 14 October. Available at: http://www.dazeddigital.com/music/article/11577/1/claire-denis-tindersticks (Accessed: 5 March 2019).

Denis, C., and Godard, A. *Trouble Every Day*. DVD, audio commentary. Rezo: 2001.

Dinning, S. (2009). 'Great Directors: Claire Denis', *Senses of Cinema* 50. Available at: http://sensesofcinema.com/2009/great-directors/claire-denis/ (Accessed: 28 February 2018).

Dufreigne, J-P. (2001). 'Elégance du cannibale,' *l'Express*, 12 July. Available at: https://www.lexpress.fr/culture/cinema/elegance-du-cannibale_643041.html (Accessed: 28 February 2018).

Eisenberg DM, Davis RB, Ettner SL, Appel S, Wilkey S, Van Rompay M, Kessler RC. Trends in alternative medicine use in the United States, 1990-1997: Results of a follow-up national survey. *JAMA*. 1998; 280(18):1569–1575.

Elley, D. (2001). 'Trouble Every Day', *Variety*, 14 May. Available at: http://variety.com/2001/film/reviews/trouble-every-day-1200468352/ (Accessed: 28 February 2018).

Film Society of Lincoln Center (2018). 'The Female Gaze', *Film Society of Lincoln Center*. Available at: https://www.youtube.com/watch?v=zh7gEuj2wCI (Accessed: 5 March 2019).

François, E. (2001). 'Trouble Every Day', *Chronic'art*, 8 July. Available at: https://www.chronicart.com/cinema/trouble-every-day/ (Accessed: 28 February 2018).

French, P. (2002). 'Trouble Every Day', *The Guardian*, 29 December. Available at: https://www.theguardian.com/film/News_Story/Critic_Review/Observer_review/0,,866031,00.html (Accessed: 28 February 2018).

Frodon, J-M. (2001). '"Il s'agit de s'aventurer au-devant d'une forme"', *Le Monde*, 11 July, p. 24.

Gaignault, F. (2017). 'Béatrice Dalle, l'interview trash d'une star du cinéma', *Marie Claire*. Available at: https://www.marieclaire.fr/,beatrice-dalle-interview-mise-a-nue-actrice-star-de-cinema,20178,22255.asp (Accessed: 28 February 2018).

Gibbons, F. and Jeffries, S. (2001). 'Cannes audience left open-mouthed', *The Guardian*, 14 May. Available at: https://www.theguardian.com/world/2001/may/14/cannes2001.cannesfilmfestival (Accessed: 28 February 2018).

Gonzalez, Y. (2001). 'Claire Denis: Murder Ballads', *Chronic'art*, 27 April. Available at: https://www.chronicart.com/digital/claire-denis-murder-ballads/ (Accessed: 28 February 2018).

Guichard, L. (2001). 'Trouble Every Day', *Télérama*, 11 Juillet.

Harrer, M-C. (2001a). 'Trouble every day: amour à mort', *Allocine*, 14 May. Available at: http://www.allocine.fr/article/fichearticle_gen_carticle=553820.html (Accessed: 28 February 2018).

Harrer, M-C. (2001b). 'Claire Denis', *Allocine*, 11 July. Available at: http://www.allocine.fr/article/fichearticle_gen_carticle=554590.html (Accessed: 28 February 2018).

Hoberman, J. (2006). 'An Actor's Revenge', *Village Voice*, February 26. Available at: https://www.villagevoice.com/2002/02/26/an-actors-revenge/ (Accessed: 28 February 2018).

Holden, S. (2002). 'Erotic Horror With Enough Gore to Distress Dracula', *New York Times*, March 1. Available at: http://www.nytimes.com/2002/03/01/movies/film-review-erotic-horror-with-enough-gore-to-distress-dracula.html (Accessed: 28 February 2018).

Hussey, A. (2010) 'Claire Denis: "For me, film-making is a journey into the impossible"', *The Guardian*, 3 July. Available at: https://www.theguardian.com/film/2010/jul/04/claire-denis-white-material-interview (Accessed: 28 February 2018).

Hynes, E. (2012). 'Claire Denis Dialogue with Eric Hynes', *Walker Art*, 17 November. Available at: https://www.youtube.com/watch?v=onYtE01KmFE (Accessed: 28 February 2018).

Indiana, G. (2018). *Vile Days The Village Voice Art Columns, 1985–1988*. South Pasadena: Semiotext(e).

Jousse, T. and Strauss F. (1994). 'Entretien avec Claire Denis', *Cahiers du cinema*, Vol. 479, pp. 25-30.

Khin, M., Cech, N. B., Kellogg, J. J., & Caesar, L. K. (2020). 'Chemical Evaluation of the Effects of Storage Conditions on the Botanical Goldenseal using Marker-based and Metabolomics Approaches', *The Yale Journal of Biology and Medicine*, 93(2), 265–275. Available at: https://www.ncbi.nlm.nih.gov/pmc/articles/PMC7309669 (Accessed: 27 May 2021).

Kristeva, J. (1982). *Powers of Horror: an essay on abjection*. Translated by Leon S. Roudiez. New York: Columbia University Press.

Lalanne, J-M. (2001). 'Quitte ou «Trouble»', *Libération*, July 11. Available at: https://next.liberation.fr/culture/2001/07/11/quitte-ou-trouble_371253 (Accessed: 28 February 2018).

LaSalle, M. (2002). 'Film Clips', *San Francisco Gate*, April 5. Available at: https://www.sfgate.com/movies/article/FILM-CLIPS-Also-opening-today-2855635.php (Accessed: 28 February 2018).

Le Vern, R. (2018). 'Claire Denis Tindersticks : trouble every film', *Chaos*, October. Available at: http://www.chaosreign.fr/claire-denis-tindersticks-trouble-every-film/ (Accessed: September 1 2019).

Lim, D. (2011). 'Symphony Space', *Artforum*, April 27. Available at: https://www.artforum.com/film/dennis-lim-on-the-tindersticks-28078 (Accessed: 28 February 2018).

M., B. de (2010). 'Exclusive interview with Claire Denis', 14 May. https://www.festival-cannes.com/en/69-editions/retrospective/2010/actualites/articles/exclusive-interview-with-claire-denis (Accessed: 28 February 2018).

Mayne, J. (2005). *Claire Denis*. Urbana: University of Illinois Press.

Met, P. (2003). 'Looking for trouble: The dialectics of lack and excess', *Kinoeye* 7 (3). Available at: http://www.kinoeye.org/03/07/met07.php (Accessed: 28 February 2018).

Musetto, V.A. (2002). 'A Film With Bite – Cannibal Tale Has Its Share Of 'Trouble'', *New York Post*, 11 February. Available at: https://nypost.com/2002/02/11/a-film-with-bite-cannibal-tale-has-its-share-of-trouble/ (Accessed: 28 February 2018).

Nancy, J. (2001). 'Icon Fury: Claire Denis's Trouble Every Day'. Translated by Douglas Morrey, 2008. *Film-Philosophy* 12 (1), pp. 1-9.

Nayman, A. (2009). 'On the Nightshift An Interview with Claire Denis', *Reverse Shot*, June 26. Available at: http://reverseshot.org/symposiums/entry/395/claire-denis(Accessed: 28 February 2018).

O'Hehir, A. (2002), 'Trouble Every Day', *Salon*, March 6. Available at: https://www.salon.com/2002/03/06/trouble_2/?_r=true (Accessed: 28 February 2018).

Péron, P. (2000). 'Claire Denis En Eau «Trouble». Aperçu Du Tournage D'un «Film D'effroi», Avec Béatrice Dalle Et Vincent Gallo', *Libération*, 8 March. Available at: https://next.liberation.fr/culture/2000/03/08/claire-denis-en-eau-trouble-apercu-du-tournage-d-un-film-d-effroi-avec-beatrice-dalle-et-vincent-gal_318881 (Accessed: 28 February 2018).

Quandt, J. (2004). 'Flesh & blood: sex and violence in recent French cinema'. *Artforum*, 42 (6), pp. 126-132.

Reid, M.A. (1996). 'Colonial observations'. *Jump Cut*, 40, pp.67-72. Available at: http://www.ejumpcut.org/archive/onlinessays/JC40folder/ClaireDenisInt.html (Accessed: 28 February 2018).

Renouard, J-P. and Wajeman, L. (2000) '"This weight of the world" interview with Claire Denis', *Vacarme*, January 2 2001. Available at: https://vacarme.org/article84.html (Accessed: 28 February 2018).

Romney, J. (2000). 'Claire Denis interviewed by Jonathan Romney', *The Guardian*, 28 June. Available at: https://www.theguardian.com/film/interview/interviewpages/0,,338784,00.html. (Accessed: 28 February 2018).

Ross, M. (2003). 'A Chance, But Not Inconsequential, Encounter: Claire Denis' "Friday Night"', *Indiewire*, 16 June. Available at: https://www.indiewire.com/2003/06/a-chance-but-not-inconsequential-encounter-claire-denis-friday-night-79660/ (Accessed: 28 February 2018).

Sanders, M. (1997). 'Vincent Gallo: mad, bad, and dangerous to know', *Dazed*, 29. Available at: http://www.dazeddigital.com/artsandculture/article/37329/1/vincent-gallo-1997-interview-buffalo-66 (Accessed: 28 February 2018).

Smith, N. (2002) 'Claire Denis Trouble Every Day', *BBC*, 24 December. Available at: http://www.bbc.co.uk/films/2002/12/24/claire_denis_trouble_every_day_interview.shtml (Accessed: 28 February 2018).

Smith, D. (2005). 'L'Intrus: An Interview with Claire Denis. *Senses of Cinema*, 35 (5). Available at: http://sensesofcinema.com/2005/conversations-with-filmmakers/claire_denis_interview/ (Accessed: 28 February 2018).

Sobchack, V. (2004). *Carnal Thoughts: Embodiment and Moving Image Culture*. Berkeley: University of California Press.

Sotinel, T. (2001). 'La Cérémonie de l'Effroi', *Le Monde*, 11 July, p. 24.

Takano, H. (2004). 'Vincent Gallo Interview'. *Free & Easy Magazine*. Audio published at: http://hikaritakano.co/index.php/audio-interviews/vincent-gallo (Accessed: 28 February 2018).

Talu, Y. (2018). 'Interview: Agnès Godard', *Film Comment*, 2 August. Available at: https://www.filmcomment.com/blog/interview-agnes-godard/ (Accessed: 5 March 2019).

Thomas, W. (2002), *Empire*, December. Available at: https://www.empireonline.com/movies/trouble-every-day/review/ (Accessed: 28 February 2018).

Vecchio, M. (2014). *The Films of Claire Denis*. London: I.B. Tauris.

Vié, C. (2002). 'Trouble Every Day: Troubles everyone'. *Fangoria*, p. 211.

Walton. S (2013). 'Enfolding Surfaces, Spaces and Materials: Claire Denis' Neo-Baroque Textures of Sensation', *Screening the Past*, 37. http://www.screeningthepast.com/2013/10/enfolding-surfaces-spaces-and-materials-claire-denis%E2%80%99-neo-baroque-textures-of-sensation/ (Accessed: 28 February 2018).

Williams, L. (1991). 'Film Bodies: Gender, Genre, and Excess', *Film Quarterly*, Vol. 44, No. 4, pp. 2-13.

Devil's Advocates

"Auteur Publishing's new Devil's Advocates critiques on individual titles offer bracingly fresh perspectives from passionate writers. The series will perfectly complement the BFI archive volumes." Christopher Fowler, Independent on Sunday

THE COMPANY OF WOLVES – JAMES GRACEY

"Gracey does his part to add to the legacy of The Company of Wolves, *strengthening the film's importance with a thoughtful monograph that is detailed and accessible, presenting arguments with deliberation and validity, never forcefully or self-righteous."* Film Int.

DAUGHTERS OF DARKNESS – KAT ELLINGER

A vampire film like no other, Daughters of Darkness *(1971) is a classic of high-Gothic cinema, loved for its art-house and erotic flavours. Kat Ellinger examines the film in the context of its contemporaries and argues for its place as an important evolutionary link in the chain of female vampire cinema.*

THE WITCH – BRANDON GRAFIUS

The first stand-alone critical study of The Witch *provides the historical and religious background necessary for a fuller appreciation, including an insight into the Puritan movement in New England, as well as situating the film within a number of horror sub-genres (such as folk horror) as well as its other literary and folkloric influences.*

www.ingramcontent.com/pod-product-compliance
Lightning Source LLC
Chambersburg PA
CBHW071413300426
44114CB00016B/2291